Dexter Isaac

Enemies Amongst Us

Funnel Vision Publishing

Enemies Amongst Us   D. Isaac

Published 2018 by Funnel Vision

Enemies Amongst Us. Copyright (c) 2018 By Dexter Isaac. All rights reserved. No part of this book may be reproduced in any form or by any electronic or mechanical means, including information storage and retrieval systems, without permission in writing from the publisher, except by a reviewer, who may quote brief passages in a review. Scanning, uploading, and electronic distribution of this book or the facilitation of such without the permission of the publisher is prohibited. Please purchase only authorized electronic versions, and do not participate in or encourage electronic piracy of copyrighted materials. Your support of the author's rights is appreciated.

This book is a work of Non-Fiction. Some of the names, characters and places have been changed In order to protect the identity and privacy of persons, living or dead connected to this story. Everything the author says is based on true events he remembers to the best of his recollections. The statue of limitations is up on most of the crimes described in this book and on the ones that's not the perpetrators are long dead, already convicted or have disappeared forever.

Cover design by Evolvinggraphics.com

For information about special discounts for bulk purchases,
please contact Funnel Vision Publishing at funnelvisionpub@gmail.com

Library of Congress Cataloging-in-Publication Data

ISBN 978-1-9841916-4-9

Dedication

This book is dedicated to two very special departed souls who I will always love and remember.

My uncle Kenny aka Kenneth Isaac aka King Hawk (R.I.P), a true Trinidadian player and the best uncle I ever had.

To Mrs. Betty Joseph Hill, (R.I.P). Although not my biological, I loved her just like she was. The best mother-in-law I ever had. You will always be in my heart.

Enemies Amongst Us   D. Isaac

Chapter 1

The time was about 12 p.m. on Friday the 26th of February, 1993. I was upstate New York serving my second prison bid in Cayuga Correctional Facility in Moravia, New York to be exact. Doing time in prison I only had a few good wise men I would seldom communicate with. On this particular day we had just finish eating lunch, and were waiting until the guards finished running chow at the mess hall so we could go to the gym and workout. When the breaking news came on the television, I was left in total shock.

"Dee. Yo Dee! Check it out! check this shit out," LA yelled, startling me, while I was drinking some Tang juice mix. Out of instinct I reached for the knife tucked in my waist band and turned his way. "Yo son, don't do that!!!" I responded after scanning the room to see him looking at the television with his hands glued to his face.

The World Trade Center had just been bombed and there could've been a lot of people dead and hundreds injured. At this time the total number of casualties was still unknown and everything was fresh. "Yo, Dex, this can't be true. This is madness. Mutha fucka!" LA exclaimed, excited from seeing such a tragic event. Shit like this doesn't happen in America, especially in New York City. "I wonder who would do some shit like that" I questioned, getting angry, and worried about the few people that I knew who worked in that area.

"The world is busy sun, we have to get out of here and get our shit together. It's time to start a family and enjoy life. Running the streets and thuggin is cool, but when all that is played out then what? Something like what we are watching happens and this turns into a third world country with us scraping the bottom of the barrel." says LA. "I wouldn't mind having a big family of my own, but raising a child around this mayhem could only be a burden. People should only have children when they are responsible and complacent in life." "Man you're right about that." "I do want some more kids though. Having a few sons to raise would be a blessing. That would be a good reason for me to do something different. I hate selling drugs and robbing people all the time. I need to do something successful and legit."

As the news continued we learned that Eyad Ismoil and Ramzi Yousef were attempting a plot to kill hundreds of thousands of Americans.

A native of Jordan, Eyad Ismoil, was the driver of a yellow rental Ryder van and the passenger of the vehicle was his friend Ramzi Yousef. In the back of the van they had a 1,336 pound (606 kg) urea nitrate-hydrogen gas enhanced bomb. This particular device had been made of a urea nitrate main charge with aluminum magnesium, having ferric oxide particles surrounding the explosive. The charge used nitroglycerine, ammonium nitrate, dynamite, smokeless powder and a fuse as booster explosives. Three tanks of bottle hydrogen were also placed in a circular configuration around the main charge, to enhance the fire ball and after burn of the solid metal particles.

During the commute to Manhattan, from Jersey City, New Jersey, Eyad and Ramzi discussed their intentions and their expectations from the explosion. While LA and I were trying to strengthen our body and minds upstate in prison they were attempting a historical attack on the land of the free.

"Eyad, when this bomb goes off, it should knock Tower One (The North Tower) into the South Tower," says Ramzi, from the passenger seat of the van. "Inshallah my brother" Eyad responded with no feelings or emotions what so ever. "When both of these towers fall, we will kill thousands of the infidels."

"We will strike a mighty blow to the great Satan and create fear in the souls of the infidel dogs" Eyad replied, parking the van in the underground garage. When the van was parked, Ramzi released his seatbelt to exit the vehicle. He then walked toward the rear of the van scanning the garage, trying not to be noticed. In the rear of the van laid a twenty foot fuse. The fuse was to be lit as the two departed the garage. When Eyad exited the vehicle he walked behind the van where Ramzi was igniting the fuse. Approximately 12:17 P.M. the bomb exploded in the underground garage, generating an estimated pressure of 150.000 psi. The explosion created a ninety eight foot wide hole through four sub-levels of concrete. The explosion shut off the World Trade Centers main electric power lines, destroying the emergency lighting system. Thick black smoke rose from the garage clouding the air as high as the 93rd floor of both towers, filling the unpressurized stairwells.

Evacuation the towers was difficult for the occupants in the buildings as they suffered from smoke inhalation injuries. The power shut off trapping hundreds inside elevators in both towers, including seventeen kindergarteners on their way down from the South Tower's observation desk. For five hours they were trapped between the 35th and 36th floors.

Getting a better understanding of the bombing I would have

Enemies Amongst Us — D. Isaac

never known I would meet someone affiliated with terrorism, let alone guess that the person I would meet would have an impact on my life causing me to spend the rest of my life in prison.

As LA and I watched more of the bombing we discussed the horror but most of the time we just let it all soak in. Instead of being in prison we could have been at one of those towers or driving down the cross streets. Life is precious without a price and everyone must find their purpose.

When the smoke cleared, the bombers had killed 6 adults and one unborn child along with 1,042 innocent civilians who were injured.

It was further reported there were 15 civilians from the blast who suffered traumatic injuries as well as an additional 20 complained about cardiac issues they were having. One of America's strong, fearless firefighters was hospitalized rescuing civilians and an EMS worker was also injured while containing the fire and subsequent aftermath.

As the news was reported across the television, LA and I discussed the matter sitting in the day room babysitting two cups of Tasters Choice coffee. While our coffee temperature fell, I found myself in a daze. Never in my life could I picture myself affiliating with anyone of such character. It would be a one in a billion chance I would meet someone that would even know the perpetrator.

Ramzi Yousef would be the cousin of Sayeed, an associate that would alter the course of my life for the worse. Through a chain of events with a best friend who is mistaken for my sister at times, Sayeed's selfishness and greed would cost him his life, while altering my life and Marilyn as well.

Chapter 2

The year was 1994. I was thirty years of age and released from prison. I had been home for about two months. I had been laying up in the house with my new wife Brenda, and I was starting to feel trapped. A beast in a cage, cooped up, playing house with Brenda.

Throughout my stay in prison, I had spoken highly on making a lot of money, and starting a family. My good friend LA had been home six months before me. I was sitting in the house listening to some Eric-B and Rakim "thinking of a master plan," when LA called.

"Yo, Dex. I'm coming to pick you up in 30 minutes, get dressed" he said when I answered the phone. "A'ight Sun, I'll be ready by the time you get here" I told him. Thirty minutes later LA called me again, "Yo, Dex meet me around the corner from your house." "A'ight" I replied suspicious of why he didn't come to the front of my house.

When I walked around the corner LA was standing at the drivers door of a clean black Chevy Suburban truck with dark tints on all the windows.

"Boy you sure know how to make my day" I yelled walking towards him, with a big smile on my face.

"It's party time," he yelled as he opened up the back door of his truck to reveal two beautiful Spanish looking women, then turning to embrace me with a nice hug showing his unconditional love for a real friend.

Enemies Amongst Us   D. Isaac

The loyalty and love was right where it needed to be. I would do anything to see LA smile and he would do the same for me. Sometimes it was like we knew what each other wanted before we received it.

As LA and I embraced. The women watched our interaction from the back of the truck. The joy on our face told the story of our connection and the ladies knew at that moment our brotherly love was genuine with the two of us.

"Ladies meet my brother from another mother. Dex this is Kelly and Katie. Ladies you two can do what ever you like to him, with him and for him. I approve" says LA as Kelly and Katie both started smiling mischievously as I climbed into the back of the truck with them.

"Boy I must say, you sure do have love for your brother" I said excitedly looking at LA as he opened the drivers door.

"So Dex, how tall are you and where are you from?" Kelly asked as I made myself comfortable.

"I'm 6' 2" and I was born on the beautiful Island of Trinidad and Tobago, but I was raised in the streets of Brooklyn, New York. I'm 250 pounds, all man and muscle. The past three years and six months I've been working out trying to get my body and mind right. What can you tell me about yourself sexy lady?" I asked, while looking at her flawless skin tone and long black hair.

"I'm from Spanish, Harlem, and these two beauties will feel better on your face" she said as she released her bra strap and pulled her shirt over her head. "I suck good, I fuck good and I will suck her while you fuck me" she said as she smiled and laid her skirt and panty on the console that separated the front seats.

"So your really going to do all that after I just told you I've been locked up in prison for three years and six months?" I asked reaching my left hand in my pants positioning my penis.

"Kelly, grab his dick for me," says Katie as she reached to loosen Kelly's bra strap. LA just sat in the drivers seat quietly as if he had planned this all out. I wasn't ashamed or insecure about nothing. Kelly pulled my dick out of my pants and started giving me a blow job while Katie undressed her. Twenty minutes later, LA drove his car into the garage of his house and we all went inside. By that time I was shirtless with my pants to my ankles. Katie and Kelly were completely naked and we all had cum at least once.

"I like your long dreads Dex" said Katie as we exited the truck and entered the house through the garage.

"I'm sure you both are going to like all this beef I have for you too. I hope you're not a vegetarian Kate?" I responded. "My favorite meat is beef" Katie replied as the festivities began.

******

"I hope you got it all out of your system" said LA as I walked down the stairs inside his house with the same smile I had when he picked me up the day before. I just laughed while flopping down on the sofa across from him.

"Man, you was fucked up at the club last night, and I heard y'all up there fucking all morning" LA stated.

"What time is it?" I asked.

"It's two thirty in the afternoon."

"Damn!"

"Yeah, but the good thing is, I have something sweet lined up for us after we go shopping."

"What are we going to do with the girls?"

"Their car is parked outside. They will go home when they are ready."

"When are they coming back?" I asked, shocked that my fun started and ended so quickly.

"Cut it out, there is a lot more where that came from. We have to get some money and get you on your feet."

"That's right. You know I appreciate you, right? These last 24 hours were amazing. I like this watch a lot. It's a knock off but we will get real ones after a few licks."

"Damn you're ungrateful," said LA with a serious tone tightening his face.

"Nah, I'm just fucking with you. We are going to ball out of control. You know you're my Dude. We don't do that. Let's go get this money then Big Dee" he said relaxing and smiling at me. "Say no more, let's get it" I said as we shook hands.

Chapter 3

It was a beautiful spring day in New York City, midway through April of 1994. After a wonderful night filled with fun and passion my reality sat in. I was thirty years of age, fresh out of prison and broke, yet I had a new wife that I had to support. Being a true Brook-nam soldier, I was down for whatever. There was no way that I was going to be on these New York streets broke for long. I resorted to what I knew best, and that is being a stick-up kid. I decided to get on my Brooklyn bullshit.

Amongst all the big time drug kingpins in the city of New York, there were quite a few trap Queens as well, that was about making that paper. Being raised in the streets, I knew a few of them. My job was to rob without rape or murder. I was known for putting in that work smoothly and as quietly as can be.

My home girl Simone, from Crown Heights, called me on my cell one afternoon. "Hey Dex, what's good with you?" she asked when I answered. "I'm good baby girl. What's up with you?" I responded.

"I'm still doing me. Just grinding."

"And what's that consist of?" I asked.

"A little of this and a little bit of that" she responded as music started playing in the back ground.

"Where the music coming from? Did you just walk into another room?" I asked out of curiosity.

"No, I turned the music on to ask you if you got anyone that I can get three bricks from. I can afford to give you a $1,000 off each one. That would be cutting into my profit but I'm not hurting."

"What they need, some boy or some girl?" I asked to see if the people buying the drugs wanted heroin or cocaine.

Enemies Amongst Us   D. Isaac

"They want that girl and they are in a rush to get back down south. Can you make something pleasant happen for me within the next couple of hours? I had someone lined up but he sold out before they arrived."

"When you get with your peoples hit me back at this number. I'm going to need about an hour to put it all in motion. I'm sure I can handle this for you" I replied with dollar signs on my mind.

"Okay, I will call you in exactly 1 hour from now. Please be at this number. This is my last time dealing with these dudes, they are in to big of a hurry and I'm not with rushing. Something could go wrong and get my ass killed or life in prison."

"I will be at this number, just hit me back. Let me go see some people and do some things and I will hit you back also."

"Thanks Dex and I'm so happy you're back. We are going to be ballin like old times."

The second I hung up the phone with Simone my brain went into overdrive. I knew when she said three bricks I was going to rob whoever she wanted to meet up with. Three bricks was three kilos and three kilos was at least sixty thousand dollars, being fresh out of prison I wasn't passing up this opportunity for nothing.

    Having the ambition of a winner and a Master's degree in Criminology. I walked to the nearest grocery store. I purchased three five pound bags of sugar and a couple rolls of green and grey masking tape.

LA had given me a thousand dollars before he had dropped me back home and it was more than enough for my first investment.

Enemies Amongst Us   D. Isaac

One of the guys I grew up with was serving ounces of cocaine up the street from my house, so I went up the street and bought six grams from him.

Running back to my residence I proceeded to make three dummy kilos of cocaine. I had some old show boxes in the house. I got three of them out of the closet, I then poured a little over half of the sugar out of each bag. One Kilo of cocaine is 2 lbs 4 ounces, and I needed to have my dummy packages in the proper weight area, so my victims wouldn't suspect anything when they got the packages in their hands.

I then took the bag with the remaining sugar and folded the shoe box around it into a tight rectangular shape and taped it together neatly. After that, I got a razorblade and cut a pyramid shaped flap on one side of the package and stuffed it with about 2 grams of real cocaine. Next, I taped the flap down with a piece of grey masking tape. Now if someone were to open the flap, they would see cocaine and think the whole package was a kilo of cocaine. I repeated the same procedure with the other two bags of sugar.

When I was finished at the house I drove over to this little bar that one of my boys worked security at on Fulton St, on the corner of Ashland Pl. in the Fort Greene area.

This bar was located two stores off the corner next to a restaurant, but it had an emergency exit in the back that let you out around the corner on Ashland Pl.

"Yo, Warren, what's good son?" I greeted him when I walked into the bar.

"Ain't nothing Dex" he replied while giving me a handshake and light hug. "What's good with you Dex? What's on you mind? You were really having a good time the other night when I saw you. I didn't even recognize you. My girl told me that was you once we got home" says Warren.

"You was at the club?"

"Yeah, I was there, I saw you with them two thick ass Spanish girls with the big tits and phat asses. You was with the boy that drive that black Suburban truck. The short bald headed American boy they call LA, but he's not from Los Angeles."

"Wow you did see me. I wish you would have said something. We have to catch up later. Aye, check it. Can you watch my back for me while I make this move?"

"Yeah I got you, don't trip" says Warren displaying his gun he had tucked under his shirt.

"I got some dudes coming in from out of town tonight that I'm looking to beat them out of their money" I told him.

"Word, son?"

"Yeah, I'm going to need to use the backdoor later on and I'm also going to need you to hold me down in case shit gets out of hand" I said.

"I got you son, just come through when your ready" he said.

"Okay! Cool. I'm going to get LA to watch my back as well. I'm going to break you off some paper when I come back."

"That's what's up. I need some extra dollars."

Enemies Amongst Us   D. Isaac

"A'ight I'mma see you later then."

We gave each other another light hug and a pat on the back, then I left.

After I left the bar, I called my road-dog LA. "What's up son? I need you to watch my back tonight" I told him.

"Do you need a burner?"

"Nah, I got my glock on me."

"Okay, I got you when and where?"

After I told him my plans for later on, and what time I needed to hook up with him, we got off the phone.

It was about 1 P.M. when Simone called me back.

"Yo Dee, I got them peoples I told you about earlier at my crib" she stated.

"Alright baby girl. I'll be there in about half an hour" I told her.

"Try to hurry Dee, because they trying to get back on the road ASAP."

"Okay Simone, I got you. Imma hurry up" I said and got off the phone with her.

I called my boy Warren to make sure he was at the bar. I then put my wife down with the move I was about to make. She was my ride-or-die chick, so she was down for whatever. I told her to park her car at the back exit of the bar on Ashland Pl. so when I came out the back exit I could jump right in the car and we could be out.

I checked myself in the mirror one last time. I put on one of my Versace shirts, some alligator shoes and jewelry with my Cartier wood frame designer glasses that cost $1,200. I had to look the part so they would feel comfortable doing business with me. This is how Rahmel had tricked me out of my $26,000 back in the days when I was with Nicole. I learned from him in a sense.

As I was about to leave my house Simone called again "Hey Dee, we left my house, meet us at Wendy's restaurant on Flatbush Ave and Empire Blvd." she said.

"Okay Ma, Imma be there in 15 minutes" I responded.

I already had Brenda and LA at the house with me so we jumped in the car and headed over to meet them.

When we pulled up to the restaurant I saw Simone's white Lexus SC300 parked in the lot. To get a better understanding on who I was dealing with, I stepped in for a burger.

"Hey Dee, what's up?" she asked as I stepped inside the restaurant. "Hey Baby girl, how are you?" I replied. "I'm good. We were just finishing up. Do you have them things with you?" "No babe. My boy is meeting us at this bar downtown with them."

There were three guys dining with Simone. They were the guys who had come up from Charlotte, North Carolina to buy the kilos of cocaine. Normally I wouldn't want my victims to know what I was driving or where I hung out, but the only thing that was on my mind was getting their money.

Simone introduced me to her friends. We agreed on $19,000 a

Enemies Amongst Us   D. Isaac

piece for the three kilos, which came to $57,000. I then told them we would have to go to my connection's bar to pick up the drugs. When LA and Brenda saw me hop in the car with Simone they drove to the meeting spot.

When we left the restaurant, I rode with Simone and one of the guys by the name of Clyde in her car. Clyde was doing all of the talking for the three guys. He acted like he was the boss of his little crew. His two friends followed behind us in their truck they had drove up in.

By the time I arrived at the bar with Simone and Clyde, everyone was already in position. Warren was on post at the door working security. LA was sitting at the bar and my wife was parked out back by the emergency exit.

Clyde went over to the truck and came back to Simone's car with a shopping bag with sixty thousand dollars inside of it and told Simone $3,000 was for her and to go with me to the bar and that they would wait across the street with the cars until we returned.

These dudes were scared to come in the bar. I was like "Damn" this is going to be easier than I thought. This shit was going to be like taking candy from a baby. When me and Simone entered the bar, the first thing I did was sat her down in a booth.

"How sweet it is to be loved by you" I said as Simone handed me the bag with the money.

"I love you too" she responded naive to the situation and flirting back with me. She had forgotten how I got down.

"A long Island ice tea for the beautiful woman and a thug

Enemies Amongst Us   D. Isaac

passion for me" I said to the bartender as we sat at the bar filled with people drinking and dancing to the loud music that was playing.

"Are you okay?" I asked Simone. "Yes. Why is this place packed so early?" she asked. "Life is a party Babe" I responded walking away from the bar area passing LA sitting on the opposite end of the bar.

I took the bag of money and told her to wait right there for me while I go to the basement office to count the money and get the drugs.

Simone was a good girl that went to college and came from a good family. She was not one of those chicken heads or hood rat girls that be in the streets, all in the mix of things. So I knew she was a little naive to the ways of the streets. I had to take advantage of that so I could get this paper.

A lot of young women get caught up with men doing crime in the streets. Most of the time they end up dead or in prison because they were looking for love in the wrong places. I knew Simone had feelings for me but all I had love for was money at this particular time in my life.

Before making my exit, I went to the back of the bar and told LA to look out for Simone and make sure she was safe. I then went out the back door and jumped into the passenger seat of Brenda's car and told her to head out to our main house on Staten Island. I now had enough money to pump up my operation in the dirty south.

Chapter 4

Things were going well down south. The women were friendly, the money was plentiful, and my living arrangement wasn't bad at all. I had a condo in North Carolina and a three bedroom house in Virginia. That was until my wife Brenda and I began constantly arguing about the decisions I was making. She was always worried that I would get arrested and sent back to prison. If it was up to me I would have bought some land down south and opened up some type of business down there. I was learning that being married sometimes you just got to let the wife make some decisions. A happy wife, a happy life.

On a return trip from down south one night, two of my boys got busted on the highway with my money and some left over drugs. The police confiscated my MPV minivan that they were driving and sent them both to jail. They placed a hold on my vehicle leaving me no choice but to leave it in their storage facility, after all the fees and penalties raked up thousands of dollars.

I decided that I needed to have a legitimate business in New York to keep me busy and to have a little income coming in until I could set up another side hustle. It was now time to go legit.

Brenda had always wanted to open up a health food store. I had a pretty penny saved up and with it being her choice, we were back in Brooklyn. I went for it! The idea would have been bad knowing small businesses were known for slow growth, but I still had other means of getting money as long as I could wrap my hands around a pistol.

Enemies Amongst Us   D. Isaac

We went and opened up D & B health Food Store in Clinton Hills on the corner of Waverly and Greene Ave, in Brooklyn.

Clinton Hills is a middle class neighborhood. It is one of the better communities in Brooklyn. There are a variety of different races and people of different ethnic origins that reside in this community. The beautiful Rosie Perez, the actress, lived two blocks over from my store. I used to wish she would stop by. The hip-hop legend Chub Rock, the rapper, lived around the corner on Washington Ave. Jeru the Damaja, another rapper and the actor who played Michael on the sitcom "Good Times" were two of my regular customers in the store. Biggie Smalls (R.I.P.) and Junior Mafia lived and hung out two more blocks over from my store. Many other actors and a few more rappers and other people in the entertainment industry lived in this area as well.

Brenda and I would work in the store from sun up to sun down. This store became my office and headquarters. I would usually work in the store until somebody called me with a jux or some type of scheme to make some extra fast money.

I was working at the store one day when I got a call on my cell.

"Dee, I got a nice jux for you. A nice sweet job, I need you to handle right away" said Katrina, a long time friend who should have found a way to make me her man years prior. Her face had a Tracie Ellis Ross glow with the exact same smile and the exact same eyes. The two even shared the same skin complexion. Katrina was just a bit thicker in all the right places. "Do you have some time for me?" she continued.

"Most definitely babe. Here's the address, come through so we can talk. I'm at the store, my wife is here so be respectful. You

Enemies Amongst Us   D. Isaac

know how she gets sometimes" I replied.

"I'm on my way give me 20 minutes."

"Kat, what color panties are you wearing?" I said with a grin, messing with her a little.

"Bye Dee, see you in twenty minutes. You play to much."

As the phone hung up I found myself deep in thought thinking about a family. At the age of 30 I had only one son from a previous relationship. Brenda and I had been having unprotected sex for years and she had never gotten pregnant. I was beginning to think that something may be wrong with her, or she might be taking some kind of birth control on the down low.

I was down in the basement getting some supplies when I heard Brenda yelling for me to come up to the front of the store. It had only been twenty minutes since the phone call with Katrina and she had arrived.

When I came upstairs Katrina was standing at the front of the store, so I introduced her to my wife hoping Brenda wouldn't start any of her jealous acting bullshit.

"Katrina this is my lovely wife Brenda. Brenda meet Katrina, she is a long time friend and business associate of mine."

"It's nice to meet you Katrina. I have heard really good things about you. I am surprised to see you here. Dex didn't tell me anyone was on their way" said Brenda with a fake smile on her face.

"Nice to meet you too. You're very pretty" said Katrina

Enemies Amongst Us　　　　　　　　D. Isaac

admiring the gorgeous Brenda, easily mistaken for the beautiful Kerry Washington everyone loves so much.

Brenda had jealousy written all over her face and Katrina knew it. All of Katrina's adornments were almost bursting out her shirt. Her thirty-six double D breasts stood up like candles on a dark stormy night and her booty followed her like a trailer as we proceeded to the rear of the store to my office where I discussed all my personal business in private.

As soon as we were in my office Katrina busted out "Yo Dee, this sucker ass Spanish dude that my home girl Melissa is fucking came by her crib talking big shit last night. You coming back to town got a bitch thinking big. Let's get this mutha fucka" said Katrina loud and excitingly as the door shut behind her.

"Damn! Calm down baby girl, what's the deal ?" I replied calmly. "Dee, check it! This mutha fucka was talking big shit trying to impress us not knowing who the fuck I am and shit. He kept going on about he got 50 kilos of coke."

"What are you saying? This Spanish mutha fucka you don't know have fifty kilos of dope somewhere waiting on us?"

"Yes, and we are going to get everyone, and do like we use to do before you left." she said, as she placed her purse on the desk and pulled the chair she sat in across the floor from me, closer to look me directly in my eyes.

"What did he say?" I asked her, my curiosity aroused. "He talked about having the fifty kilos of cocaine." "Coke?" I interrupted her excitedly. "Yes, coke, cocaine and he said he has some country dudes coming up from down south somewhere in

Virginia to pick up all fifty at nineteen thousand a brick in a couple of days. I don't know why son was boasting like that but he did what he did and we are going to do what we do." "Line it up baby girl, and we are going to get both of them. Matter of fact who is this dude?" "Some Puerto Rican tight pants, curly hair, slim dude." she said. "And now that I think back on it, son reminds me of a Puerto Rican Bruno Mars with his fly pretty boy swag." As I sat there digesting what Katrina had just told me while doing the math in my head, I realized that she was talking about damn near a million dollars worth of drugs. My dick started getting hard as U.S steel thinking about all that free money. Being the business minded person that I am, my mind started going crazy trying to figure out how I could kill two birds with one stone. It sure would be nice to catch them together when they was doing the transaction, so I could get the money and the drugs. But I knew that would have been to much to hope for. But if I could do both, I could go back down south to the Carolina's and never look back.

"Hey Dee I got the info on this dude for you." Katrina said bringing me back into focus. "Tell me what you got ma." "He lives on the first floor of this brownstone house on Bond street between Bergen and Wyckoff with this light skin chick name Jessica." "What else?" I asked "He drives a blue 850i BMW and a silver 525i BMW. His girlfriend drives a burgundy Nissan Pathfinder truck and she goes to some college downtown Brooklyn during the daytime."

"That's it baby girl?" I asked. "Nah, they got mad jewelry too, he be blinged out all the time wearing big ass diamonds in his ears and they be rocking his and hers Rolex watches, mink coats and all types of shit, this dude be ballin Dee" she stated looking me directly in my eyes.

Enemies Amongst Us   D. Isaac

While sitting in my office digesting all the information Katrina was telling me, I knew she was serious. Baby girl was a down ass chick when it came to getting money. She thought and behaved just like a dude when it came to hustling in them streets. Katrina was about her business. Her and her girlfriends were very high maintenance. They did not fuck with broke dudes, they only messed with ballers and big drug dealers that were moving serious weight. The average drug dealer on the corner couldn't get the time of day from these chicks. Sometimes they would have dudes on the street corners selling drugs for them.

"I'm going to get with Melissa in an hour to ease drop on her conversation and I will keep you updated on what I learn." she said picking up her purse to leave my office.

Before leaving the store she had a short conversation with Brenda about some thing's only women discuss from what I know. What I did learn about the conversation is that Brenda gained her security becoming more comfortable when Katrina began coming around with her adornments out. They had an understanding and they both knew their positions in my life.

After Katrina completed her conversation with Brenda I walked her outside to her new Mercedes truck. I then told her that I would call her as soon as I got the job done and break her off with some money for hooking me up with the jux. I stood outside for a minute shaking my head as I watched her drive off blasting a song about she don't want no scrubs, because they can't do nothing for her by the group "TLC".

I didn't have to tell Katrina that I was going to give her some money. She knew this already. That's just how it works in the streets. One hand washes the other. I had a bunch of female friends throughout the city just like Katrina. They would go out and have sex with ballers and drug dealers and then set them up for me to rob, whenever they felt like the dudes were trying to play them or if they felt like he was a sucker.

At the time I was driving a new white Toyota Land Cruiser truck and I also bought a Ford Taurus car that I had a stash box installed in to keep my guns in. I had the windows of the Taurus tinted out dark, so nobody could see inside it when I was out creeping on fools. The Taurus was my working car. Back in my office, I called up my boy LA and told him to come meet me at my store and that I had a jux for us to go check out.

Three hours later, as I sat talking to LA and Shameek, my two goons about the jux, Katrina called. She had discovered more insight on KK. When I told her I had sat down with the big people she knew it was a go. The big people was actually two little people who became giants with sixteen in the clip and one in the hole. LA wasn't no bigger than NBA star Nate Robinson and Shameek reminded me a lot of Marshawn "Beast Mode" Lynch with some nice three-sixty waves and an attitude when things didn't go his way.

After I finished talking to LA and Shameek, I told Brenda that I would be back in a little while and we left in the Taurus to go check out where KK lived. The block that he lived on was on a one-way traffic street with some light foot traffic on it. It was located around the corner from the Gowanus Housing Projects. After we had scoped out the neighborhood for a while, we headed back to my office so we could figure out how we was going to pull off this robbery. "Yo son, this shit is close as a mutha fucka to your spot" LA stated as he was settling into a chair in my office. "Yeah I know, I'm going to have to ski mask up for this one son" I said.

"Shit this nigga lives like 5 minutes from your store Dee." "I know, that's why I can't let him see my face." "You might just have to sit in the car and watch out for the po-po while me and Shameek do this one son" LA then said. "I was just thinking the same thing also, but shit we gonna play it by ear when the time comes" I said. "Well, son we have to do this once a week until I get on my feet." says Shameek.

"Yo, son I need a couple hundred thousand" says LA. "Be patient. We are going to be good" I told them.

"I can't wait, it's been so long since I seen the fear of death in a sucker's eyes praying to the game God he makes it till tomorrow" says Shameek, pointing his gun at the mirror on the bathroom door inside my shop.

"Put that up son, you're wilding" I said laughing at him practicing being hard like he's in Hollywood competing with Denzel or somebody on Training Day.

"Yo, Dee, you're going to have to sit this one out we don't want to take any unnecessary chances" said LA. Then I kissed Brenda good night handing her the keys to our Toyota Land Cruiser.

When night fell, LA, Shameek and I parked on the block down the street form KK's house so we could watch and see if we could catch him or his girlfriend slipping so we could gain access to their apartment.

While we staked out on the block, Katrina called me on my cell. "Hey, Dee, where the fuck you at?" she asked. "Girl, I ain't

Enemies Amongst Us   D. Isaac

your mutha fuckin' man, why the fuck you calling me questioning me?" I snapped at her. Katrina started laughing on the phone in my ear, "Nah baby, I didn't mean it like that" she said. "Okay, then what's up?" "I'm just calling to tell you KK is at Melissa's house and he is getting ready to take her out to eat at the Shark Bar in the city, and after that, they are going over to party at the Q-Club out in Queens." "That's good looking out babe, because I'm parked on the nigga's block right now waiting on his ass to come home. I'm sorry for snapping at you" I said. "Boy you know I don't pay you no mind, I'm happy that you're on your hungry shit, I like that. You know I love you" she said. "I love you too girl and I will talk to you tomorrow" I said as I got off the phone with her.

   When I got off the phone, both LA and Shameek were staring at me. "What the fuck y'all looking at me like that for?" I snapped at them.

   "We love you too Dread" they both replied laughing at me.

   See, this is why it ain't good to be talking that love stuff to your woman in front of your boys because they will clown your ass.

   I wanted to get a look at KK so we drove over to Melissa's block to see if we could get a peep at him, but by the time we had gotten there they had already left. We then decided to go to the Q-club to pick up the trail. When we got to the club I circled the area because we didn't see his car. By the time we made it back to the front of the club one of the club's bouncers was moving some cones that were in the street, in front of the club so KK could park his car.

   "Yo, son check this mutha fucka out, he got reserved parking directly in front of the club like he's the mutha fucking owner or something" LA stated as we sat there watching KK park his 850i BMW.

He pulled up like he was Frank Lucas or Nicky Barnes in the 70's when they ran the city. When he got out of the car he was wearing a mink jacket opened up in the front to show off his jewelry. Shameek said "homeboy stuntin' real hard son. I knew right then and there without a doubt in my mind that we were going to get his bitch ass. While we were sitting in the car outside the club Katrina called again. "What's up baby? What are you doing now?" she asked me.

"Call me daddy. I'm too much of a man to be a baby. What's the matter you miss me or something?" I asked flirting with her. "Yeah, I miss that big black dick you got waiting on me after we take care of this business" she teased back. "Girl what color panties you wearing?" I asked. "Boy stop playing with me before I tell Brenda on your ass" she said. "What the hell do you want then?" I asked her.

"I'm just calling to tell you that I just talked to Melissa and she said that KK was spending the night at her house and that he wasn't going home tonight, so don't be out there wasting your time waiting on him all night." Thanks baby girl" I told her and got off the phone with her.

We cut our vigil of him short and went home to catch a few hours rest.

Chapter 5

The following morning my wife Brenda made sure the neighbors smelled the breakfast she was cooking. Smoke filled the house and I filled her mouth. She either had something to prove or she was feeling horny the way she was pleasuring me. No hands no teeth as she wrapped her mouth around me.

The phone is ringing, are you going to get that?" I asked as my toes curled and eyes closed while enjoying the pleasure she was giving me. "No. It's just Marylyn. She called earlier." Brenda responded drooling out her mouth using her left cheek to hold my shaft on my stomach, positioning to put my balls in her mouth.

"What she want?" I asked trying to take my mind off of the pleasure forcing me to bust a nut all over Brenda's beautiful face. I didn't want to cum too fast. Married men don't get pleased like this all the time. "She said she have something lined up for you." Brenda spoke as she choked on two weeks of backed up sperm. "Aah!" I said relieving myself ejaculating everything in me all over her face. "Thank you baby." I said expressing my appreciation. "You're welcome. Tell Katrina thanks, she inspired that." "What!" "Yeah she can't have you, that dick is mine. She don't have to try I know my husband. He is ambitious and eager . He will go get what he needs as well as what he wants." she replied washing the cum from her face and out of her hair.

That wasn't a conversation for me to entertain. I stood up with my dick in my hand ready for round two. I had been trying to make

Enemies Amongst Us   D. Isaac

a baby since my release from prison.

"Gimmie that dick daddy" she said bending over the bed grabbing both her cheeks opening up the gates to heaven.

"Say no more" I said sliding my dick into her dripping wet pussy. "This pussy wet and tight baby" I said going deep into her. "Slow daddy" she said complaining like it was our first time. Little did she know I didn't like all that complaining shit. Ten pound babies almost two feet in length comes out of a woman, how much damage could I do with a 9 inch dick.

"Take this dick and shut up" I said beating her pussy up like a real porn star. "Don't ever let two weeks go by and you don't give daddy none of this good juicy wet pussy" I said as she apologized moaning, Cumming and crying accepting all my frustration.

"Do you think I don't deserve this pussy or something? Or do you think this dick is too good for you? I married you. You married me. Sex is a huge part of this commitment. You hear me?"

"Yes, daddy I hear you" she said Cumming for the third time.

"Turn around." I demanded. Get on your knees"

"Matter of fact, lay on your back and put your legs behind your head" I demanded

"She did as I insisted and I pounded in that pussy, dripping every drop in her. I wanted a baby and all the build up had to be some kind of help after two weeks.

I loved my wife but I loved my money more. Breakfast was delicious, the sex was off the hook, and the day was beautiful. I had to get to the money. Marilyn could only be calling early in the morning to lay some good news on me.

****

Marilyn was another one of my female associates. She was like a sister to me. I would do anything for her and she would do the same for me. Real-estate was her profession and she met a lot of big ballers doing what she does. A lot of her clients would hit on her sexually, both men and women. She was that fine. I had my moments with her but we were better off just doing business and being friends. She reminded me of the actress Angela Bassett. Same complexion, same smile. I called her back after I had finished making love to my wife.

"What's up Marilyn? Brenda told me you called" I said, when she answered her phone.

"Hey, Dee there's a spot in Flatbush I want you to look into when you have some free time" she said.

"Okay, I'm on it. What's the address?" I asked.

"I gave the address to your wife. This Nigerian from Africa became very disrespectful with me after I denied his sexual advancements. I didn't want to tell my boyfriend. I want you to hurt his pocket not his body" she said turning me loose on his bitch ass.

"Okay, he has that coming, you know I got your back. I'm going to make him regret ever disrespecting you" I replied.

"Okay thanks. Keep me posted."

"Before you get off the phone, how is your relationship going with that new man of yours?" I asked her.

"Believe it or not we just left Las Vegas. I loved every moment of it. From the lights to the fights, the gambling, the shows, everything. Las Vegas has every culture food you could name. It was an amazing week" she replied sounding happier than ever.

"That's wonderful I wouldn't expect nothing but the best for you. If he ever gets out of line call me and I will set his ass straight" I told her.

"That's why I love you Dee. I will keep you posted if he ever acts up and also on the African. If I get anymore information I will let you know."

"Okay, I'm going to check things out" I told her ending the call.

My hand was forced to rob the Nigerian Prince but that had to wait until I got KK and Jessica out of the way. Fifty kilos of cocaine would be enough to kick back for some time. Marilyn needed me to punish this African bastard. The Nigerian robbery was a must do jux. I would have to let LA and Shameek know about this new plan.

Chapter 6

"Your boy is out front" Brenda told me while talking on the phone to one of her friends. LA was on the other line.

"Okay" I told her, giving her a kiss then putting on my bullet proof vest and grabbing my Ruger P89 and an extra 19 shot clip heading out the door. Approaching the Suburban truck LA and Shameek were driving, I couldn't do anything but thank the Lord above for such a beautiful day. The sky was clear, the wind was calm and I could smell money in the air. By 8:00 AM we were back on KK's block watching the entrance to their apartment.

"Yo, Son, get ready somebody coming out of their crib" LA said.

"Damn, she's fine as a mutha fucka" Shameek blurted out.

"Yeah, she's even prettier than Melissa, this dude must be crazy cheating on her, then again she probably isn't as freaky as Melissa" I said.

"You know Dee, some of these pretty girls ain't shit in the bed some of them can't fuck worth a damn" LA stated. "Yeah, I know what you're saying, I done came across a few like that" I said.

"As we were watching the house Jessica came outside. She was about 5'8" with long black hair that came down a little ways past her shoulders, light skinned complexion with a sexy figure like the actress Paula Patton. "As we watched her, she slammed the gate to

Enemies Amongst Us   D. Isaac

their house without locking it like she was angry about something. She then jumped into her truck and sped off down the street like a bat out of hell. Before I could get the words out my mouth LA and Shameek yelled out, "she's going to jail." We laughed all the while with our eyes on the prize.

"Yo Son, looks like she mad at KK for staying out all night" I said bringing to our attention that KK must still be in the house. "Shameek let's go Son this is our chance, she left the door open. Dee you stay back and watch out in case something transpires" LA stated as the two of them exited the car.

Being parked nearly six or seven house from where KK lived I could see it would take maybe thirty seconds to step foot inside his door. Moments before LA and Shameek approached the house next door to KK's, Jessica pulled back in front of the house and ran back inside like she had forgotten something while leaving the gate and door to their apartment wide open. As she stormed in, LA and Shameek creeped in right behind her closing the apartment door, locking it shut to pursue the robbery.

"BANG, Click" went the door and the lock as LA grabbed Jessica wrapping his left arm around her covering her mouth with his hand.

"Don't make this out to be more than what it is" said Shameek standing in front of LA and Jessica staring into his eyes.

"We don't want to kill you or your dude we just want the money and drugs and we will leave quietly. If you want to make this bigger than what it is I can show you how an explosion looks" Shameek told her, pointing his gun at Jessica touching her beautiful face with the barrel of the gun.

Enemies Amongst Us   D. Isaac

The two sat Jessica on the sofa in the living room and began tying her hands and feet together. One strip of duct tape covered her mouth with a bandana over her eyes.

"Does he have a gun?" Shameek asked a very frightened Jessica. Shaking her head no the tears poured down her face.

"Don't move or I will kill you" Shameek said striking more fear into her heart before going into the room where KK lay sleeping still hung over from partying all night with Melissa.

"Wake yo bitch ass up" Shameek said as LA stood over KK with his gun pointed at his forehead.

"This is what partying all night gets you sucka. Do you think you can just run around Brooklyn stuntin without any consequences?" LA asked, as piss ran down KK's thigh wetting the bed.

"What's this? What's up? What you guys want from me?" KK asked, as he laid there vulnerable and weak.

"Turn over bitch" LA ordered cocking his desert eagle, leaning over towards KK letting him look down the barrel. "This can go easy or it can go hard. We have your bitch in the living room tied up. We can fuck her up and beat you half to death then find what we came for or you can keep your appearance and she can keep her sanity, just tell me where it's at" says Shameek mean mugging him.

"001 this is 007 is everything good out there?" LA asked speaking into his walkie talkie. "Yeah 007 everything is good out here, everything good with you?" I responded. "It's all secure in here, we are about to look for this cheddar. Let me hit you when we are ready to come out" he responded, before going to pursue the robbery quick and easy as possible.

"Bitch boy my dick getting hard and I been wanting to fuck your bitch all night. I don't think you want that, do you?" asked Shameek as KK shook his head no with water coming out his eyes like a little bitch.

Jessica sat quietly on the sofa in the living room while LA and Shameek finished duct taping KK and confining him to his hall closet. On the hunt for the fifty kilos of cocaine the two overlooked a lot of small compact area where thousands of dollars could easily be tucked away safely.

After minutes of ransacking the apartment LA and Shameek decided to call it quits and hit me on their walkie talkie. The two were angry. They had only found an ounce of cocaine.

"001 this is 007 we are coming out. Are we good?" asked LA. "I'm pulling up to the front come out" I responded sitting up in the car placing it in gear and speeding to the front of the house.

"Yo, this is some bullshit" said Shameek as he jumped in the backseat with a large black trash bag, slamming his door after LA jumped in the front seat.

"That was easy but we didn't get no fucking fifty kilos of cocaine. I grabbed maybe, an ounce he had for recreational purposes, some money, like ten grand, and some jewelry, but that's it." said LA.

"For just a couple days of work we still did good. He must have a stash house or another spot. I'm quite sure he's probably going to try and lay low for a while. That's when we'll surprise him again" I said."Word" said LA and Shameek at the same time.

Enemies Amongst Us   D. Isaac

"Word. I have another jux lined up already don't be discouraged. If it's meant for us we are going to get it, we just have to do what we do. That's rob sucka ass niggas who think they are stuntin." said Shameek as he counted the money and checked out the jewelry.

"Did you loosen up the tape so one of them could break loose?" LA asked Shameek. "I hope he did." I said. "Yes and I started to French kiss that chick pretty ass. Yo I'm gonna hit that one day" said Shameek.

When pulling jack moves there can be many surprises. The best robbers are the ones with a conscious. They tend to be the ones who play it smart and get away. My crew only wanted the money we didn't want any further attention, and we weren't trying to go do any unnecessary time behind bars.

****

Hours later Katrina pulled up on me at the store. LA and Shameek had gone off to go sell the jewelry and the drugs. The smile on her face told a story that hadn't been written yet. She had received a call from Melissa informing her about the robbery with the assumption we had taken the fifty kilos of cocaine.

"What's up beautiful lady?" I said, as the bell on the door rang and I opened the door.

"Hey Big Daddy" she said, running into my arms hugging me like she hadn't seen me in ages.

"Oh I get a kiss now" I joked as her lips left mines.

Enemies Amongst Us								D. Isaac

"I told you I was going to give you some of these goodies when you were finished."

"My wife can hear you" I replied with a shocked look on my face.

"What?" she gasped in a panicked state waiting for Brenda to walk out from the back.

"I'm just fucking with you. What brought you over here so early?" I asked, cracking up laughing at her.

"Melissa called and told me something and I assumed something and.......what did y'all get?"

"All bad with some good." I replied shaking my head.

"Dee, y'all ain't find no drugs at all?" she asked me after I'd told her we didn't find none like she couldn't believe it.

"Nah, baby girl we didn't find shit."

"Dee tell me you at least got all their jewelry right?" she asked. "We got some Jewelry, but not much." "Did you at least get their Rolex watches and all of Jessica's diamond jewelry?" "Nah babe none of that stuff was in the apartment."

Katrina almost blew a blood vessel cussing when I told her that, slamming her hand on the counter. After she had calmed down she said "Yo Dee, they must be keeping all their stuff at Jessica's mother's apartment in Flatbush."

"Yeah, he might be doing that baby girl." "Imma get the address for you" she said. "Alright Ma you do that" as we said our good byes.

Enemies Amongst Us   D. Isaac

    When LA and Shameek went to the jewelry store that we usually did business with to sell the jewels we had taken we found out most of KK's jewelry was fake. The two big diamond stud earrings he was wearing in his ears were cubic zirconium. The diamond tester didn't even make a beep and the needle didn't even move. This dude was fronting with glass in his ears. The gold chain around his neck was fake but the diamond on it was real, so I kept that for myself.

    Later on when I went home, I went up to Brenda and I put the cross on the chain that I had taken from the Tupac robbery that I had given her to wear. LA, Shameek and Katrina split up the money and the rest of the jewelry we had sold. I was so disgusted by the outcome of the robbery I didn't want any of it.

Chapter 7

After pulling off the robbery at KK's house, it was now time to do a favor for my good friend Marilyn. She had given me the address along with the time to expect the Nigerian to be home. Flatbush was my new come up. I was also waiting patiently for Katrina to call me with Jessica's mother's address. I was undecided about which robbery I wanted to do first. I didn't like the fact that the Nigerian was disrespectful to Marilyn, so I decided I was going to rob him first.

Marilyn told me the Nigerian was named Hakeem, and he lived on the sixth floor of this big apartment building located on Clarkson Ave. in the Flatbush section of Brooklyn. Every morning he would leave his house at about 9:30 and drive over to 5th Ave in Park Slope in his green Acura Legend Coupe to open his real-estate office.

I had been watching Hakeem for about 2 weeks on and off getting his routine down pat before I made a move on him. This dude was a big black, bald headed mutha fucka. He was about 6'3" and a solid 270 lbs. He was always dressed very conservatively in suits or dress slacks with shirts and shoes. He was not flashy like a lot of other drug dealers in the city. He did not wear loud jewelry or hangout in clubs all night partying.

This dude was real smooth with his movements and if Marilyn hadn't put me on to him, I never would of known he was a drug dealer just by looking at him. I would have taken him for just another hard working real-estate agent and that's exactly what he wanted everybody to think of him, while he was selling his poison

Enemies Amongst Us   D. Isaac

to other drug dealers.

   I watched him from my car while he was hanging out at his real-estate office. When he got a call from one of his drug customers, he drove back to his apartment on Clarkson Ave, got the drugs and met his customer a few blocks from his house and did the transaction in the car, on one of the side streets in his neighborhood.

   Selling heroin in bulk or weight is a lot different than selling cocaine the same way. For one, heroin is a lot more expensive than cocaine. Where as cocaine is between $16,000 to $20,000 depending on droughts in the city or who you knew. A kilo of heroin was worth about $110,000 to $200,000 depending on the quality and who you were dealing with.

   In New York City the dealers and users of heroin loved the dope known as China White. This particular brand is known as the best heroin in the world and is imported from China. The Nigerians were starting to import their own heroin and were becoming major playas in the dope game. You didn't see heroin known as tar or Mexican mud in NYC like you do on the West Coast. Being that heroin was so expensive to buy in bulk compared to cocaine and crack, that is one of the reasons you didn't see too many young black heroin dealers compared to cocaine dealers. Heroin is also very tricky to handle, if someone didn't know what they were doing mixing it up, they could mess up the product and lose all the money they had paid for it. There is no such thing as a refund once you touched the product. This is another reason why you didn't see too many young blacks in the ghettos selling heroin. This is another reason the Africans were able to fly below the radar of the police and the stick-up kids of the city. People selling heroin in

Enemies Amongst Us   D. Isaac

bulk did not get much traffic. Their customers were few and they were consistent. A person selling heroin in bulk might only have 5 to 10 regular customers that they did business with. The customers didn't buy from them everyday or at the same times like cocaine or crack addicts. Selling heroin in bulk is usually a low key smooth operation and that's exactly what the African had going on as I observed him.

   To be a good stick up kid, I learned to have patience, that came with studying the people I was going to rob as much as I can. This is called doing your homework in my trade and I took it very seriously.

    From studying the African hustlers in NYC there were two things I learned about them. One was that they were some greedy and selfish people. They did not like sharing their money with their friends and they did not like to carry guns in America for some reason.

   The African I was plotting on was very sneaky. I realized one day that he was not sleeping at the apartment on Clarkson Ave every night as I first thought. On the weekends and on some weeknights he didn't even sleep there at all. I decided to step up my surveillance on him and put LA and Shameek on to the jux.

   "What up son?" LA answered his phone, with Method Man bumping in the background. "Yo turn that shit down I got something to tell you" I responded. "What's good?" he asked as the music faded. "Look I need you and Shameek to meet me at the health food store" "Ok, Imma go grab him up and meet you in twenty. I gotta drop my girl off and use her car so make that thirty minutes" he replied. "A'ight Son, Imma see you there" I said

Enemies Amongst Us					D. Isaac

ending the call.

*****

The weather was perfect for short pants, a polo top and my favorite butter timbs. I stood with my left boot on the wall of D&B health foods while waiting for LA and Shameek to pull up. Walking along the opposite side of the street I noticed a childhood friend I had mad love and respect for growing up.

"Yo, JD what's good fool?" I yelled at my boy throwing my hands in the air and walking towards the curb. "Yo, Dee! What's happening with you?" he responded crossing the street. "Brenda was working this store when I came by the other day with my aunt" JD said pointing at the D&B sign. "Son, I'm good. Brenda is my wife. We got married while I was in prison" I said. "Yeah? I heard you was down. Three years is a long time."

"Yo, you look bad what you been doing with your life?" "I been living here and there. Things been rough for me since you left. I haven't hit no jux or nothing. I been existing, this shit sucks Dread. What you up to?" he asked noticing the new clothes I was wearing.

"Yo, as long as all the malls and 5th Ave is open I'm going to do some shopping, I spoke lifting my foot back on the wall. Check it, if you can stay here a minute I'm going to holla at my boys and I'm gonna put you on this jux we got lined up. Stay here." I ordered as I walked to LA's car.

"What's up fellas?" I asked, greeting LA and Shameek as I took a seat in the car. "What's good yo?" they asked looking at JD pacing in front of my store. "Who's that dude?" asked Shameek. "This dude I grew up with. I want to put him on our next jux, help

Enemies Amongst Us   D. Isaac

put some funds in his pocket. What ya'll think?"

"Son, he on some kind of dope?" LA asked watching JD twitching. "Some kind of hard drugs." Shameek added.

"I'm gonna give him some paper and I'll be right back." I said as I stepped out of the car and handed JD a c-note.

When living the street life you learn how to fish and you teach how to fish before you give a fish. I would of been helping him fish by bringing him along. Not really though because I was robbing and stealing with him when we were children. I would call it burglarizing but its all stealing when your taking something that isn't yours. My aspirations were big, I wanted to be successful and my definition of success was having money. They say money is the root of all evil but what they don't say is money is the key to many doors.

After I broke JD off and wished him well I jumped in the drivers seat of LA's girl's ride and smashed off. It was time to get some money. Marilyn had put me on the moves Hakeem was making and I wanted my cut. I still had nightmares about the fifty kilos, the little Puerto Rican KK, was supposed to have and it reminded me of the ground I needed to make up.

"This busta has heroin and coke from what Marilyn said" I explained. "We really need this lick to be clean and easy. One kilo of each would have us sitting pretty. He is supposed to have 10 each" I added, driving towards Hakeem's spot. "We gotta get it this time." Shameek said. "We need to focus, then when the time is right we are gonna move in" I responded as I pulled the car over a little ways down Hakeem's block.

Enemies Amongst Us

D. Isaac

Sitting patiently waiting for Hakeem to leave his office for lunch and head home to grab his duffel bag I explained to LA and Shameek exactly what was gonna happen. I told them what he was going to be wearing, where he would park, where he would put the duffel bag, how long he would be in the house even the way he would look before he got in his car to drive off.

Just like every weekday Hakeem pulled up to his house at 12:20 in the afternoon, stayed in his house ten minutes. came out with a duffel bag, placed it in his back seat and looked across the street towards the building on the corner from his car before closing his door and pulling into traffic. The man was consistent if anything and I had him down pat.

"So where is he going?" LA asked curious about exactly how much I knew. "Curiosity killed the cat." I replied sharply. "Do you even know?" Shameek piped in. "Of course." I responded. "Well why aren't we heading there?" LA asked.

"We will hit his spot and his girls spot. What we don't get here we will get there and if we are not sitting fat by then we can always hit his office. He makes 5 to 10 sales a day there too."

"Yo, son this is the one." Shameek said excitedly. "Yo! You even have his girls information, good work." says LA bigging me up.

"Let's get this money boys" I replied thinking to myself how a person can never be too safe. This guy flew under many radars while operating right in front of our face. The police didn't see him, the jack boys missed him, this was a low key, smooth operator with a big time operation. He was also now my marquee victim.

Enemies Amongst Us

D. Isaac

The plan was to walk into his building before he entered. However that changed once I explained exactly what he was gonna do. Luckily he doubled back into his apartment for something, giving us the time we needed to get into the building before he could run back out.

Once inside the building, the elevator opened for the four of us to enter. We all loaded into the elevator, him none the wiser to what fate had in store for him. He pressed the button for the 6th floor and I reached around and pressed the 7th floor not wanting to reveal my intentions till absolutely necessary.

I have to give it to him he showed no fear seeing us dressed in black sharing the elevator with him. He either had a set of balls or was way too comfortable in his security.

"Today's your lucky day." I said pulling out and putting my Ruger P89 to the right side of his head. "Don't make a fucking sound. Just go to your door and open it" LA said as the elevator stopped with a "DING" on his floor.

"Third door." I said pointing to his apartment as Shameek patted him down. "Okay, Okay, just don't kill me" he whimpered as he fumbled with his key in the lock. Once inside we laid him face down on the living room floor and stripped him butt naked, before duct taping his hands and ankles.

The first thing a good jack boy does during a home invasion is secure the premises, and that's exactly what Shameek, and LA set off to do. When they gave me the all clear I told Shameek to go to the car we can handle it from here. That way our get away ride would be waiting as soon as we finished.

Enemies Amongst Us					D. Isaac

Shameek left as LA and I started tearing up the apartment like a fed raid. Leaving no cushion unturned or drawer unopened searching for money and dope.

"007 this is 001 are you ready" I said into the walkie talkie, after a few minutes of searching. "007 is waiting on you boss" Shameek replied.

LA came into the room holding up a duffel bag and said "let's go."

I loosened the duct tape so Hakeem could eventually wiggle his way free and we called for Shameek on the radio.

"007, your wait is over, we on our way." then left the apartment for the elevator.

The ride down seemed longer than it probably was but leaving the scene of a crime fully armed and carrying the evidence can take a toll on even the coolest operators' nerves. All that tension was completely unnecessary considering we didn't see one person on our trip down from the apartment to the car.

"I already grabbed the bag from his car" Shameek said, as we hopped in the waiting car. It seemed that the day itself had gotten so much brighter. "I don't know about anyone else, but I want to go get some nice shit from 5th Ave for Brenda, my mom and some shit for my son as well. A little celebration can never hurt anyone" I said as I checked out the bundles of cash and the brown bag of beige powder, I saw LA find under the kitchen sink then smile as he loaded it into the duffel bag.

The jux was successful and we laughed as we confirmed everything was there. The money totaled $40,000, and the dope

Enemies Amongst Us   D. Isaac

was a half kilo of pure uncut heroin. The dope and money got split three ways after I took out $5,000 for Marilyn. The jewelry got pieced out and I ended up with a couple gold chains that I put up for a rainy day.

Chapter 8

About a week later Katrina called and gave me Jessica's mother's address, so I drove out to Flatbush to check out her building and neighborhood that she lived in. Jessica's mother lived with her other daughter, Jessica's younger sister. They lived in a big apartment on the first floor of a building on Woodruff Ave. right off the corner on a quiet side street behind Prospect park. There was not much traffic on this street and I found the Pathfinder, Jessica's truck, parked on this block.

About two weeks after the robbery on Bond Street, while me and the boys were riding around looking for something to rob, guess who we saw? "Yo, son look at that cutie in the pathfinder over there" my boy JD said. "Oh shit !!! That's Jessica" LA said in the seat next me. Sure enough when I looked over, I saw Jessica in her truck right next to us driving up Flatbush Ave coming from downtown Brooklyn. It was about 1 PM in the afternoon and she was heading in the direction of her mother's house. I hit the gas and left her on Flatbush Ave as I beat her to her mother's block.

"Yo, JD you and Shameek take one of these walkie talkies and go ring the bells in front of the building and get somebody to buzz y'all in and go in and wait for her on the second floor. I'll call you on the radio and let you know when she enters the building" I told them. "We got you son" they both replied exiting the car and heading to their positions.

It was as if the game lord wanted this to happen. Soon as JD and Shameek walked toward the door someone exited the building and they were able to gain access before the door closed.

Enemies Amongst Us   D. Isaac

"002 this is 001, when she comes into the building take her at the door of her apartment " I advised, hoping to avoid a scene in the hallway. "10-4 we on it boss" JD responded through the walkie talkie.

As LA and I waited in the car Jessica pulled up, parked and headed into the building.

"002 she in coming your way" I radioed them. "10-4" said JD. I then turned on the police scanner I kept in the car so I would have a heads up if the po-po caught on to what was about to transpire.

When Jessica seen JD standing in her hallway she knew what time it was before he ever pulled his gun. He put the pistol to her head as Shameek emerged from the stairwell and the 3 of them entered the apartment. "Everybody face down" Shameek yelled as JD shoved Jessica to the ground. "Don't make a fucking sound" JD added, sweeping his pistol across the room until it found Jessica's mother and stopping on her.

They duct taped both Jessica and her mother and found the little sister in the bedroom when securing the house. With all three duct taped on the kitchen floor they radioed. "001 send in 007 we need an extra hand. Three vics are all in here and all is secure." "Buzz him in. He's in route" I said as LA exited the car. That's why he was my number one. He knew when he was needed and didn't need to be instructed.

Once inside LA took over, he left JD to watch the three vics while him and Shameek started searching for the stash. They were flipping over mattresses and ripping out drawers in a bedroom when they heard a struggle coming from the kitchen where JD was watching the vics.

Enemies Amongst Us   D. Isaac

LA went to see what the racket was and caught JD trying to pull down Jessica's pants noticing she wasn't wearing any panties. "Yo, son, what the fuck you think your doing?" He snapped. Still tugging her pants JD responded "Yo man, she fine as a mutha fucka I'm trying to hit that." "Nigga is you crazy? We don't play that shit, we ain't here for that leave her the fuck alone." LA called me on the radio "001 this is 007, your man in here trying to turn this into a rape situation, you need to talk to him" he said angrily. "Hold on 1 sec." I responded as I caught a glimpse of KK running out of the building towards Flatbush with a cell phone in his hands. I couldn't believe my eyes. "Yo 007, grab whatever y'all can get and get the fuck out of there. I just seen KK come out of the building running down the block" I said into the radio. "On our way son" he replied.

I pulled the car up to the curb as the three of them came out the building ,LA carrying 2 black garbage bags, and jumped in the ride as I drove off. "How the fuck did y'all let KK get away?" I screamed and hit the steering wheel in frustration. "He wasn't there. He wasn't in the apartment" Shameek responded. "Well where the fuck did he come from, Mars?"

"Yo we don't fucking know" they all said. "And JD, what the fuck you was doing trying to take some pussy during the job" I asked him, furious that he behaved that way. "We're professionals and that is not how professionals act" I screamed. He just looked at me all dumb like, he knew I was mad. JD was my boy and I had mad love for him, we went way back, but everyone in the car knew that shit was unacceptable. I'm sure he knew if he was someone else I woulda just shot him and been done with it. He had embarrassed the shit out of me, after I spoke for him, giving him a chance, he pulled a stunt like that. I was happy LA had caught him before he had violated Jessica like that, and I made a decision,

Enemies Amongst Us   D. Isaac

since I was not going to shoot him I was also not going to give him shit from the robbery.

"I'm not gonna kill you for this" I explained "so be grateful for not getting a bullet. However your not getting shit else either" I told him. He started to argue and I cut him short. "Say one more word and I might change my mind about the bullet." That kept him silent the rest of the ride to his house.

After dropping him off at his house we went back to my stash house to split up the loot. Once again we didn't find any drugs. All they had taken was some jewelry and three mink coats. I was sick KK had gotten away again, I was starting to think he had a horseshoe stuck up his ass to get away from my crew, once was unheard of. To slide by twice and only lose a few G's was impossible.

Later, after I'd calmed down a little, we drove into the city to the garment district to see what we could get for the minks. Just when I thought things couldn't get any worse we were informed that the coats were made from male minks and cheaper than if they were made from female minks. The furrier didn't even want to buy them from us. I had to take them by my boy's barber shop in Brooklyn and luckily he took me to his mother's house and she hesitantly coughed up $4,500 for the three of them. Still it was better than nothing but I was starting to take this KK thing personally, and was wondering if he was even worth my time.

Also we still missed the Rolex watches and whatever diamonds Katrina was talking about. I was so frustrated with the situation that I was ready to just go to Linden Plaza and shoot him in the face on G.P (General Principal) for faking so hard and wasting our

Enemies Amongst Us   D. Isaac

time.

    Later in life I even found out that the cars he was driving were rentals from this car dealer named Leroy. Leroy rented exotic cars to drug dealers and hustlers all over Brooklyn. If you wanted to rent a Benz, BMW, Porsche, Lexus you name it Leroy would get it for you if your money was right. Just another way KK was faking hard as a mutha fucka

Chapter 9

Unbeknownst to us Shameek was friends with a cat named Tut who lived around his hood in East New York. After we did robberies, Shameek would go back to his hood and brag about the lick to Tut trying to impress him. Well Tut had a little reputation as a stick up kid himself, and liked to go around bragging about all the robberies he did trying to build up his street cred.

Tut's bragging caught up to him one summer at a BBQ when KK's cousin heard him bragging about how he had robbed KK and Jessica. Tut was at the BBQ bragging about the robbery like it was his work, when in fact he was nowhere around and had never done any robberies with our crew. However due to Shameek's mouth Tut knew intimate details about some of the jobs we did and laid claim to them, trying to pump up his image. KK's cousin called him and told him that Tut had been bragging and boasting about robbing him. When KK heard this he proved what we already thought, he was faking like turkey bacon. He put the cops on Tut and got him locked up rather than dealing with the problem and busting a cap inTut himself like any real G would do.

To make matters worse Jessica went to court and perjured herself when she testified and pointed Tut out in the courtroom saying he was the one that robbed them, and even raped her. She knew she was never raped by him or anybody else. There was no DNA samples, police or hospital reports about the rape. Still the U.S. attorney , Karen Monroe, sat Jessica up there and led her through the rehearsed and coached lies. The outcome was an innocent man being sent to prison for life. The combination of his mouth and a thirsty, dirty prosecutor trying to build her portfolio cost this man his freedom, for the rest of his days.

   Tut was found guilty at his trial in court mainly due to Tiffany's testimony. He was sentenced to life in prison for Conspiracy to distribute 50 kilos of cocaine and home invasion robbery. The sad thing is that he wasn't even there nor did he get a dime of the money from either of the robberies. What's even worse was there was never any cocaine at all. KK was fronting to entrap real drug dealers for the DEA, and using his clout to impress females so he could fuck them. What's even crazier is KK is still running around the streets of Brooklyn 23 years later doing the same shit. While Tut rots away in the Federal Prison.

   In 2009 some lying ass Ex-NYPD detective with a hard on for Haitian Jack wrote some bullshit about how Jack and Tut kicked in KKs door, stole his stash and threatened Jessica to keep her from testifying. I was so disgusted by that bullshit when I read it I had to write this chapter of my book to expose his fraudulent ass. If brothers and sisters on lockdown were to start picking up pens and paper instead of spending so much time in front of the idiot box AKA television and shed some light on these corrupt so called officials, maybe things like this wouldn't happen as much. The tactics of some of these vindictive cops and prosecutors out there trying to make a name for themselves in quite unbelievable.

   Haitian Jack AKA Jacques Agnant and King Tut was nowhere near the vicinity both times we ran up on KK and Jessica's spot. Yet this lying ass ex-cop would rather have people believe his bullshit like it was the gospel, even if it cost an innocent man decades of incarceration.

Chapter 9

I was relaxing in the Jacuzzi at the Jade East motel on the corner of Rockaway Blvd and South Conduit Ave in Queens, NY with one of my side chicks, Nikkia when my friend Marilyn called me on my cell-phone. Marilyn and I had endless love for each other, far beyond the typical boyfriend and girlfriend relationship. We truly loved each other like brother and sister.

Marilyn had migrated from the island of Haiti to the United States in the mid 70's, like myself and many other foreigners during that time. She came for a piece of the American dream and this is how she found it.

Marilyn came to America on a work visa and found work as a home attendant, cooking, washing clothes, and scrubbing floors for the elderly and the rich. At night she attended school to further her education and better herself. It was never her intention to live the lifestyle that she did. She had left her daughter and only child with her mother in Haiti and intended to make enough money to send home to help her impoverished family while still supporting herself.

As time passed she applied, and was granted American citizenship in the U.S. Marilyn was a woman with a plan, hardworking, strong minded and independent. Eventually she found a job working as a real-estate agent for a small office in the West Indian community in the Flatbush section of Brooklyn.

Marilyn took to real-estate like a fish to water, she was a

natural salesperson. She was about 5'7", caramel complexion with long wavy hair that came down to the middle of her back. She was extremely charming and could light up an entire room like a thousand watt light bulb with a simple smile. People loved her and eventually she became very successful in the real estate market.

"Good morning to you" Marilyn said, filled with energy despite the hour being so early.

"Bonjour cherie, allez-vous?" (hello beautiful, how are you) I responded speaking French like a true Mack. "I'm fine Dee" she said, excited I was learning to speak her native tongue. "What are you doing?" she asked. "I'm at a motel laid up with one of my ladies" "Come by the real estate office when you're done. I need to holla at you about some things." "Okay Babe, I'll see you in a couple hours" I said, ending the call and returning to the dime piece on my side.

Marilyn's main real estate office was in the Park Slope section of Brooklyn on 5th Ave. She had bought several houses throughout the boroughs of NYC and made a decent, legal, living renting them to her fellow immigrants as they came to the country and needed a roof over their heads as they chased their version of the American dream. By the mid 90's Marilyn was a successful independent woman and found herself lacking one thing, love. She wanted a man in her life to love and be loved by so she could feel complete.

Chapter 11

My Baby Mama had dropped my son off with me for a week, which slowed all my business down but gave me the chance to play daddy.

My sons name is Davon and he was 5 years young at the time. He was always the happiest riding around with me in the truck. He would bob his head as the music blasted, and imitate me as we cruised the streets of Brooklyn.

One morning we were driving to B's Restaurant on Fulton St. to get some breakfast, when I noticed a Jamaican Rasta looking like new money. This cat was looking like MR.T with all the gold Jewelry he was wearing. He was Gucci down from head to toe just like Biggie said, "rings and watches, down to the socks". As my brain and eyes locked in on him all I could hear is "ching ching" like a cash register opening in my head.

My son noticed me watching him and asked, "Daddy who is that?"

"That's free money waiting on me to come make a withdrawal."I replied with a smile.

He looked at me, then the Rasta and duplicated my smile perfectly. It's amazing how observant kids can be.

"Listen son, I want you to always remember this. "Nobody can give you freedom. Nobody can give you equality or justice or anything. If your a real man, you take it" I explained, quoting the great Malcolm X.

Enemies Amongst Us   D. Isaac

Over the next few days I would take my son with me to case the Rasta. Some might say that I was a bad dad but I was spending quality time with my son, while plotting how we were gonna eat, and I didn't see anything wrong with that. Plus no one would ever suspect anything if they saw me creeping with a kid in the car.

One day while we were on a stake out, I asked my son "What you want to be when you grow up?"

He bit his lip and thought about it for a second then looked me right in the eye and said, " I want to be just like you and mama daddy."

I was confused, not sure what he meant so I asked, "What do you mean?"

"Well you is a gangsta daddy and my mother is a rapper, so I guess I wanna be a gangsta rapper when I grow up." He explained with a serious, determined look on his face.

From watching the Jamaican Rasta I learned that he had a couple of weed spots through-out Brooklyn where people hustled for him. He was about 5'9", dark skinned complexion with long dread locks reaching his waist. He resembles the actor that played Screw Face in the movie "Marked for Death" which starred the actor Steven Segal.

At the time Fulton St. between Bedford and Franklin AVE's was known as the biggest drug block in Brooklyn. You could get anything from a $5. bag of weed to a 100 pounds or any amount of cocaine, crack, heroin, even guns. It was wide open. You had to be a real gangsta to hustle on this block or anywhere in the vicinity, and if you was not known to bust your gun or have killers on your

Enemies Amongst Us   D. Isaac

payroll you might as well keep pushing cause you had no place on this block.

   I had peeped the Rasta a few times while I was cruising around Brooklyn with my son. A true jack boy is always aware of his surroundings and it couldn't be a coincidence that every time I saw this dude he was on a known drug block. Also I picked up he drove a black 735i BMW with chromed out blades, low-profile tires and tinted windows. So when I seen him coming out of the weed spot on Fulton St. with a big brown bag in his hands, walking with swag like he was the baddest mutha fucka on the planet. Obviously he was doing things, but what he didn't seem to know is he was doing them in my town, and I wanted my cut so I decided to follow him for a bit and see what he was really about. My Baby Mama had picked up my son a couple days before so I was able to step up my surveillance.

   After he left the spot on Fulton St. he drove over to Nostrand Ave. between ST. Johns Place and sterling Place in Crown Heights to another known weed block and Rastafarian hang-out. On this block I observed him go into the trunk of his car and come out with another brown bag, before going into another weed spot. I watched and he didn't leave me waiting but a few minutes before he came back out, obviously he was making his rounds.

   From there he drove down Nostrand Ave. out to the Flatbush area where he parked on Hawthorne Ave between Flatbush AVE and Bedford Ave. He took a couple shopping bags out of his trunk and entered an apartment building.

   It went on like this as I followed this sucka for about three days all over Brooklyn and back without him being any wiser. He had a simple routine and would leave his apartment on Hawthorne Ave every morning at about 11AM. He would be driving around dropping off weed and collecting money till about 2 PM when he'd return home.

The Rasta moved with confidence and swag, like he thought that nobody had the nerve to rob him. So he didn't suspect shit when LA and Shameek rolled into his building behind him. All he saw was two clean cut Yankee boys coming into his building and probably quickly dismissed them as a threat.

When they got off the elevator on the same floor as him, they both pulled their straps "Don't move a muscle starr or I'ma splatter your brains all over the wall." LA told him as he cocked the hammer of his big ugly black .357 magnum back, and pointed the barrel at his head. Shameek quickly searched the Rasta making sure he had no weapons and ready to disarm him if he found one.

"Don't shoot, don't kill me, please don't kill me." the Rasta begged for his life as all the Screw Face arrogance went right out of him.

That big ugly gun LA carried like the actor Clint Eastwood used in the "Dirty Harry" seemed to have that effect even on the badest mutha fuckas.

"Man, this ain't worth it, please don't kill me" The Rasta kept saying as he shook his head from side to side.

"We'll decide that." Shameek snapped then added "How many people in your apartment?"

"Just my two little children, please don't hurt them. I'll give you everything I have." He begged tears starting to form in his eyes.

Enemies Amongst Us						D. Isaac

"Play if you want, but I will kill you." Shameek explained and nudged in the apartment door with his .9mm Browning

Once inside the spot they quickly duct taped him and the two kids making sure the apartment was secure. The kids was watching Popeye the Sailor man when they entered the apartment . The Rasta had two kids, a girl about 10 and boy about 8.

This dude was breaking one of the cardinal rules of hustling. He was shitting where he ate and that's a big no-no in the dope game. If your gonna sell drugs, you never bring that shit where you and your family reside. The wife and children are supposed to be secure and free from all the drama involved in the game. My man the late Biggie Smalls (RIP) rapped about this in his song "The Ten Crack Commandments." You have to rent a stash house or at least a storage unit for that exact purpose. Never mix the two no matter the cost. The Rasta was being irresponsible, cheap, and reckless by keeping his marijuana and money where his wife and kids slept.

After the apartment was secure LA hit me on the radio. "001 we straight on your end?"

"Yeah Baby Boy we all good out here." I responded, leaning back in my seat keeping my eye on the entrance of the building.

He then asked the Rasta where the stash was at, which he quickly coughed up. All he kept saying was, "Don't hurt me Pickneys brethren." over and over until Shameek got so sick of it he yelled.

"Say that shit one more time and I'll pistol whip you till you stop."

What this fool didn't know is not only were we professionals but we were also parents and weren't into hurting little kids, no matter the situation. Plus it wasn't their fault their daddy was a dumbass. We would've fucked his ass up in a heart beat but never would've laid a hand on the kids.

He ended up having about $17,000 in cash laying around and 12 pounds of that chocolate weed. Combined with a few gold chains and rings ,that we took to my boy in Albee square mall downtown, it turned out to be a decent lick.

Chapter 12

About a month after we had robbed the Rasta it was time to find another mark. Not looking for one I was just in my car sitting back bumping Biggie Smalls "juicy" on repeat when Katrina hit me on my cell.

"What's up baby? You don't love me no more?" She asked.

"You know your my girl for life, of course I do." I replied.

"Then why haven't you called? You don't want any of this bomb ass pussy?" she asked.

"I just been chilling Baby." I explained "You know I'm always in need of anything free." I finished with a chuckle to get a rise out of her.

"I know that's right, you and me both. I need to holla at you about something, you busy?" she asked.

Enemies Amongst Us — D. Isaac

"Come on girl, you know I ain't never to busy for you. Why don't you swing by my store and pick me up, then we can go downtown to Junior's and get some of that cheesecake you love while we talk it over." I sweet talked her.

"Aight, sounds good Big Daddy, I'll be there in 15 minutes." she said, ending our conversation.

A few minutes later, Katrina pulled up in her truck in front of my store and unlocked the passenger door so I could hop in. We shared a hug and skipped the small talk as she immediately starting venting about her relationship with her husband Carlos. Carlos was a immigrant from Colombia who had been moving major weight to the U.S. and wanted to remain in the land of milk and honey. Katrina was fed up with his selfishness and inconsideration.

As we pulled into the Albee Square mall's parking lot behind Junior's restaurant she expressed to me how Carlos should be the next big jux. She wanted him robbed and she wanted it done now. Her anger towards him grew as our conversation progressed. The expansion of our conversation told me I was on the right side of this friendship. I was shocked she would get her own husband robbed, and possibly kidnapped and beaten. The agreement Katrina and Carlos shared was strictly business to help Carlos with citizenship. Once she married Carlos she caught feelings, turning business into a love affair which was not a part of their plan, and never a good idea. They began having random sex which became a distraction along with the money he would give her from time to time or when she would ask.

$10,000 and a wedding ring paid for Katrina's services, yet her greedy ass wasn't satisfied with that. She got nosey and learned how much money he was really making moving dope with his brother. So here she was trying to justify her bullshit by telling me Carlos was messing with some young fly Spanish chick from south America. She rambled on how he was still her husband and that he was trying to play her. I'm a business man first and her friend second, so I listened as she vented but the whole time my money was on the score. Like Biggie says "Gimmie the loot, Gimmie the loot."

"Fuck that Dee." she smiled at me "I'm married to him still and I need mines."

"Girl you know this is crazy right?" I asked.

"Dee, I ain't no punk bitch. I ain't crazy and this shit ain't crazy. This is money, and lots of it." she replied any trace of a smile wiped from her face as she stared me in the eyes. Of all people she knew how to get my attention and soon as she brought up money she had it.

"Your husband though?" I asked.

"Yes Dee. Now are you going to let me tell you about this jux or keep playing marriage counselor?"

"Your right baby girl, go head."

"Alright now listen, they own a bar on 5th AVE. in Park Slope. My hubby runs it, a lot of Columbians come here to drink and pick up blow from them. His brother handles those transactions."

"They keep the dope at the bar?" I asked, my interest peaking.

"No they have a stash spot, an apartment on the first floor in a

Enemies Amongst Us   D. Isaac

two family house in Bushwick on Covert St. off Wilson Ave. That's where the coke's at."

"Dee I saw it with my own eyes. They got duffel bags and suitcases full of cocaine in there. I'm talking a couple hundred ki's Dee and this mutha fucka only gave me $10,000 and a lame ass ring to marry his ass, allowing him to stay in the country and get rich. Now he's got the nerve to be fucking some Latina slut? Fuck that shit, we're going to rob his bitch ass."

"Okay baby, it's on you, it's your call." I conceded.

It was on and popping once she gave me the inside scoop on the operation. I started casing the fool hours after our conversation and waited for him or his brother to slip so I could make my move.

After watching the house the Colombians occupied on Covert St. for about three weeks my patience began to wear thin. I couldn't get the ups on them and irritations started to wear on me. That move me into another direction with one of my other boys who goes by the name of Buddy. We set up the time and place for a robbery he had lined up and our victim was a no show. That angered me even more. That drove me back to Covert Street to see if I could get lucky and catch Carlos brother slipping one Saturday night.

LA, Shameek, Buddy and I were like four hungry wolves on the hunt for something to eat. As we sat in my car laying on Carlos brother's house Buddy let me know he had Dre and Sly sitting down the street in his car waiting on us to give them the word or signal to move in. That made us six deep on the creep.

"Yo Son, the other day I went to get some breakfast at Mike's

Enemies Amongst Us   D. Isaac

Diner on the corner of Dekalb Ave and St James Place and guess who I see in there Slippin?" I said.

"Who Son ?" Shameek asked.

"That Nigga Jay-Z. He was up in there early in the morning with two bad bitches and no security."

"Word son ? Why didn't you call me so we could of bagged his ass ?" LA said.

" Man you know Mikes Diner is just down the block from the 88 Precinct and the Police and all them college kids from Pratt institute be all up in there." I responded.

"Man so what, We could have followed him home or something."

"Man I didn't want to get him cause he is the Homie and he getting ready to blow up and do something positive with his life. Plus he only had on one small chain."

" What was he driving ? Shameek asked?"

"This money green Range Rover.

After we had been waiting on the block laying for an hour, the Colombian pulled up in front of the house driving a Dodge Caravan all of a sudden.

"Yo Son, It's Christmas time in the city. There he goes right there in that Caravan." I said out loud, excited.

"And it looks like he is dressed to impress. He looks like he's going on a date or out to party or something." LA said, as him and

Shameek excited the car and started walking up the street towards the house to intercept him.

"I'm going to my car to get my walkie talkie, hit me when you need me to move in." Buddy says, as he walked to his car to put Dre and Sly on point.

I had to give it to the Colombian he could dress real nice. He was wearing a shinny light blue sharkskin two piece suit. I could see the bling he was wearing around his neck, wrist and fingers from down the street sitting in my car.

"Yo 004, this is 001," I hit Buddy on his walkie talkie when I saw him enter his car.

"What's up 001 ?" he responded.

"Showtime, 007 and 006 is on the move, hold them down in the front of the crib." I directed Buddy.

"I got you," He replied.

As I watched, LA and Shameek ran up on the Colombian as he opened the front door to enter the house. After about two minutes Buddy went into the house behind them instead of staying outside like I had told him to do. Three minutes after that they all came running back out of the house. LA and Shameek jumps into my car and tells me to drive while Buddy runs to his car and drives off.

While driving I noticed that LA and Shameek were very angry and I became upset as well as they explained what had transpired inside of the apartment.

The Colombian was in the process of opening the door to his

Enemies Amongst Us   D. Isaac

apartment on the first floor for them when he said "Just don't kill me please, I will give you everything." He had begged for his life after the sight of the first gun and began to faint when he noticed the second trained on his dome piece. "$100,000 is nothing. I'll give you that and 200 kilos of cocaine." He told them. That was moments before Buddy walked into the lobby of the building.

At the same time an innocent young boy about five years old that lived on the second floor above the Columbian, comes out on the upstairs landing and sees them with their guns out and says, " Hi "to them wanting them to play with him. Buddy's dumb ass points his gun at the kid and scares him. The kid bolts and Buddy is forced to chase him up the stairs and into an open apartment door, where he encounters a whole family.

The family upstairs was completely oblivious to what was going on in the apartment downstairs until Buddy burst into their residence waving his gun like a maniac. He looked around and realized he couldn't contain the whole family himself so again he panicked and fled their apartment and ran back downstairs. Thus fucking up the whole jux for all of us.

After LA and Shameek told me how the Columbian told them that 200 kilos was nothing to him I wanted to cry. The three of us wanted to shoot Buddy for fucking up the jux of a life time. I had to use all the restraint I could muster and gave him a pass cause we went way back. Thinking back on that night we all would have been straight after that robbery had Buddy just kept his dumbass outside like I'd told him. Well you know what they say "Good help is hard to find." what they don't say is it's especially hard to find on the wrong side of the law.

Chapter 13

Sayeed Mohammed was born in a country located on the northwestern coast of the Persian Gulf known as Kuwait in the mid 1950's. He claimed to be the cousin of the terrorist know as Ramzi Yousef. And just like his famous cousin he followed in his footsteps and spent time at Al-Qaeda training camps in Afghanistan.

Some would call Sayeed a Muslim Fundamentalist. He hated America and everything it stood for with a passion, he prayed constantly for it's destruction and swore that some day he would do everything in his power to see that happen.

Sayeed came to America in the early 1990's on a forged passport just like a lot of other terrorist did around that time. Instead of staying in Jersey City, New Jersey with his cousin Ramzi, Sayeed moved to Brooklyn, New York at a childhood friend's apartment. He wanted to distance himself from his cousin and the other terrorist cell that was staying in New Jersey.

Sayeed did not come to America to partake in the actual bombing of the World Trade Center. His mission or orders was to secure housing and supply clothing and transportation for other Al-Qaeda members when they came to the United States. Not every member of a terrorist group was suicidal or was part of the actual bombing group. There was different jobs for all of the members. Like in all military or Para-Military group there are people assigned to different functions like reconnaissance, intelligence gathering,

Enemies Amongst Us   D. Isaac

transportation, funding and partaking in the actual assaults. Sayeed had his job to do and he intended to do it well.

Shortly after the bombing of the World Trade Center in 1993, A friend of Sayeed's took him to Marilyn's real-estate office in Flatbush so he could rent an apartment. Marilyn found him a nice two bedroom apartment in the Borough park section of Brooklyn. This friend of Sayeed's knew Marilyn from doing business with her in the past and they had become friends, he also knew that Marilyn was single so he played match maker and hooked Sayeed and Marilyn up together.

Sayeed was about 6'1" 190 lbs with a tan complexion from being out in the hot sun in the Middle East all of his life. He had pearly white teeth and was quite charming when he wanted to be. He poured on the charm on Marilyn and he quickly seduced her after a few dates. Marilyn fell in love with Sayeed very fast without taking the proper time to really get to know him, she thought that she had finally found Mr. Right. The man of her dreams. Boy was she sadly mistaken.

****

About a month after the botched robbery, LA and Shameek went out to Queen to rob some Dominican drug dealer at his home. Some dude name Shaborn that Shameek had befriended and he thought he knew had set up the robbery. I didn't have a clue who this dude was so when Shameek mentioned the job to me, I shunned him. I was never a fan of robbing with people I didn't

Enemies Amongst Us

D. Isaac

know. I wasn't familiar with Shaborn's work and all money is not good money. That's the motto that I lived by and Shaborn was a stranger to me.

Shaborn hyped Shameek and LA up by telling them that the Dominican kept a couple hundred kilos of cocaine in his house with his wife and children. When they heard that they knew the Dominican would give up everything once they entered his house waving their guns and got the drop on him. The house didn't have and security alarms and the dude didn't have any bodyguards from what Shaborn said to really put a battery in Shameek and LA's back. So off they went to do the job with him.

The had plans was for Shaborn to stay outside and watch out for the police while Shameek and LA entered the house. Not much was in the house after it was all said and done, but before LA and Shameek could look for anything, LA's sixth sense told him something wasn't right. As he looked out the window of the living room inside the house he heard sirens from police cars. And there were about thirty police officers outside the premises and more on the way. Shaborn had set them up. Unbeknown to them Shaborn had already caught a drug case and he had decided to co-orperate with the DEA to maintain his freedom.

Shaborn had set my Boys up. After spotting the police they dropped everything they had bagged up to take with them and took off through the back door before the cops could surround the entire neighborhood. Shameek was caught in a neighbor's backyard while LA escaped.

Two weeks later while Shameek was being held at the Queens House Of Detention, he made a call to LA and asked him to come

Enemies Amongst Us   D. Isaac

and visit him and bring him some money for commissary. Being the loyal friend LA was he did what was asked of him. I would of done the same if I was LA thinking there was nothing wrong with that and keeping it real. The visit went well, they discussed everything about the robbery. On the way out of the Detention Center while walking to his car, LA was rushed by several of the local NYPD officers.

When he was searched the cops of course found nothing on his person, but they searched the area until they found his car where they would find his Smith & Wession .357 Magnum. LA was taken into custody and they impounded his car immediately.

While LA awaited sentencing on Rikers Island he called me and told me what had happened to him.

"Dee, What's good my Brother?" He said when I accepted his collect call.

"Ain't nothing Son. How are you holding up?" I responded.

"Yo, I'm good, but I need you to bring me some sneakers and some money."

"Okay, no problem I can get that to you ASAP."

"I need you to come visit me Dee. I have to share somethings with you." He said,

When he said that I immediately thought back to how he ended up in jail. Hmmmm??? I said to myself. Now he wants me to do the same dumb shit he did that got him jammed up.

"How about I send your girl to come see you and bring you some money and the sneakers." I said.

"You good Son, I'm going to see you later." He said, ensuring me I didn't have anything to worry about. So what I did I do ? I went and visit my Dogg. I was a little skeptical at first but I eventually said fuck it and made it happen.

As I sat visiting with LA he told me he was taking everything well but Shameek had been going crazy being caged up. Shameek's behavior had changed drastically while awaiting sentencing. He would argue, fuss and fight to get his point across about the littlest of things. He would even threaten the guards if things didn't go his way. LA was chill though. He was ready to go do his time and get situated in prison and get this shit over with.

When their sentencing time came around Shameek hadn't changed a bit. He started tripping going crazy in the courtroom cussing at the Judge and Prosecutors out. He told the Judge he didn't give a fuck and he could sentence them both to the maximum sentence. LA quickly intervened when he heard him say that and told the Judge that Shameek was not speaking for him and that he had nothing to do with what Shameek was saying. He began to apologizing to the Judge expressing his remorse and asking to be sentenced separately from Shameek.

The Judge ended up Sentencing Shameek to 25 years and LA to 10 years. And I was at a lost of my two road Doggs.

Enemies Amongst Us   D. Isaac

Chapter 14

   Life didn't stop when my boys LA and Shameek went away to prison, the hustle had to keep going. As a real hustler I just had to adapt. Even though I'd miss my Doggs LA and Shameek and the jux we would come up on life goes on. Plus someone had to keep their books laced while they were away.

   Shortly after they went away, I started hanging out with my friend named Squeeze. Squeeze was a good dude and lived in Flatbush with his mother and younger sister in a 2 family house. They had the top floor which consisted of a 3 bedroom apartment for themselves. Squeeze was about 5' 8" light skinned complexion, slim built with curly hair. He was what some would call one of them pretty boy types.

   Squeeze introduced me to the check and credit card fraud game. He had developed a system in which to rip-off the banks out of their money without using any guns or violence. He would order blank business checks from these office supply places and with the use of his Dell computer and a scanner he would duplicate other company checks that he would get. The key to this process was the use of the magnetic ink which he used on the bottom of the checks when he typed in the bank accounts and routing numbers. Magnetic ink is what the banks use to verify the authenticity of the check and clear funds for payment.

   We both had friends that worked in different mail rooms in big companies such as Wal-Mart, Fed Ex, Merrill Lynch and Home Depot just to name a few. All they had to do was copy any checks they came across that was made out for over $20,000 dollars and

Enemies Amongst Us   D. Isaac

give it to us and we would pay them a couple hundred for their services.

Once we had the copy of the check we would then call the 1-800 number for the bank that the account belonged to and see how much money was available in the account. All we had to do was ask if the account was good to pay a check for $20,000 and we would know how much we had to work with, We never took all of the money from the account because this would have drawn a red flag to the bank. The next step was to duplicate the signature on the check and my boy Squeeze was a master forger.

While all this was going on we would also be having girls opening up checking and savings accounts in banks all over the city. If a check came from Citibank or Chase Manhattan Bank we would open up dummy accounts in those banks, because since the money was going into an account within the same bank, the banks policy was to credit the account with the money within 24 hours after the check was deposited in the account. Once the money became available we would then drive the girls all over the city to banks withdrawing the money a couple thousand at a time so as not to draw attention to the account by withdrawing a larger amount. If you went into a bank and withdraw over $10,000 in cash the bank teller would call the bank manager and they would have you fill out the IRS forms and we didn't need that attention.

I didn't know it all but I knew that Squeeze would give me all the ins and outs. We were destined for millions and were on the road to riches and success. It was time to work.

"Dee, once we withdraw most of the money from this account we are going to pay these girls and drop them off at the mall to do some shopping for themselves and us." Squeeze said, one day while we was out on the grind.

"I'm with you Playa. I'm down with whatever it takes to keep this money coming in. If you want we can take this show on the road. I wouldn't mind spending a month in California or Nevada. Los Angles and Las Vegas sounds real good right about now." I responded

"We aren't going to give the girls to much cash neither. We are going to let them spend the checks on anything they want, shoes, clothes, and jewelry, whatever they want."

"Shit I need some of that for my wife and my son as well." I said, excited that I wasn't going to come out my pocket with any cash.

The girls were covered and well secured if anything went wrong. Squeeze and I were always waiting outside the door weather it was a bank or a department store when they were cashing checks. They used fake I.D.'s with the card holders info, but a picture of them. Without a criminal record they couldn't be found even with use of their fingerprint.

Credit cards were a little different. We had to recruit people that worked in the Post office who delivered the mail. You couldn't just approach every mail person you saw on the streets asking them to sell you credit cards. Tampering with the U.S. mail is federal offense and could get you 20 years in Federal prison. You had to choose who you approached wisely or you would have the Feds on your ass very quickly.

We eventually recruited a few people in the employment of the post office. Extra money always appeals to people and that's the angle we took. We would pay anywhere from $100-$150 per credit card or income tax return checks. That is if the checks were over $1,500.

Cashing the income tax checks was easy for us because I had a couple of friends that worked at different check cashing establishments through out the five boroughs. All I had to do was send one of their girlfriends into the store when they were working and they would cash all of the checks for me. I'd take out whatever the checks cost me then split the rest. Well almost split it. I led them all to believe that I was paying $300 for every check. Fuck, every little bit helps right?

One day I was in the city's diamond district on 47th St. and was looking to buy some jewelry. I happened to run into one of my homies, Peanut, from Trinidad that I had grown up with in Flatbush. He was hustling people on the block. His hustle was hanging on the block looking for people coming through trying to sell stolen jewelry. Peanut knew every crooked jeweler in the city, he knew who would buy stolen goods. who was paying the highest price that day everything. Being that the price of gold changes daily, Peanut used that to his advantage. Whenever he'd bring a customer to the jeweler they'd automatically rig the price on the the piece so Peanut would get a decent cut. For example say they were buying gold at $12. per penny weight, they would tell you it was $8. and peanut would get his 30 percent off the top. It was all pretty smooth cause who would complain about not getting face value for stolen goods?

After me and Peanut finished catching up on old times and had told each other what we had going on in our lives he asked me "Yo Dread, so what you doing on this block anyway?"

"I'm looking to treat myself to a couple pieces of nice jewelry Son, why else would I be here?" I replied.

"How you plan on paying for it?"

"Cash."

"You buggin' son," He stated looking at me like I had lost my mind.

"Why you say that Nut?"

"Why would you pay for jewelry with cash when you could use them fake checks you and your people be printing? "

I stared at Peanut as my brain went into overdrive as I digested what he had said to me. Why hadn't I thought of that myself?

"Yo, Dread, I got this greedy Spanish jeweler lined up we could run game on with them checks."

"Word?"

"Yeah, this mutha fucka jerked me outta some loot and I want to repay the favor."

"Okay." I say, my curiosity spiked "Lets hear your plan."

"When we go into the store I'm going to introduce you as a rapper and tell him you my peeps and your looking to buy some Rolex's for your squad." He said.

"Which rapper?" I asked liking his plan.

"Lord Jamal from the group "Brand Nubians." There is three of them in that group, and he isn't going to know what they look like

Enemies Amongst Us   D. Isaac

anyway. Anyway you do look a little like him with the dread and ya'll about the same complexion. Only difference is you just a little bigger." He said.

 I thought it through and had to hand it to him. For being made up on the spot the plot made sense. He wouldn't know what this dude looked like and would be eager to not only make the initial sale but hopefully gain a future account of just one rapper but his entire crew.

 The jeweler Peanut took me to was none other than Tito. The same jeweler Jimmy and I had bought out jewelry from back in 1990 when we were robbing all them Colombian and Dominican drug dealers rounding up the loot for him to open Henchman Entertainment.

 Luckily, when Peanut introduced me, Tito didn't recognize me. I don't know if it was cause of the muscle I had put on in prison, the Cartier sunglasses that hid most of my face, the dreadlocks I didn't have before, or just to many years and customers to remember me, but the important part was he didn't.

 "Tito this is my mans Lord Jamal from the rap group "Brand Nubians" " Peanut explained introducing me to the owner of the jewelry store. "He wants to get some pieces for him and his crew so treat him right. He's a friend from back in the day." He finished.

 "Not a problem, not a problem." Tito said reaching for and shaking my hand "A friend of yours is a friend of mine. Obviously pleased to be in the presence of a big name rapper.

 Walking around the display case to show me what he had in stock he conversationally asked "And how have you been Peanut?"

Enemies Amongst Us   D. Isaac

giving him a sly wink thinking they had a sucker on the hook.

"I'm good thanks for asking." He replied then added "Make sure you give my boy a good deal, show him some love." acting like he wouldn't say that for anyone he brought in there.

"No problem, you know I'll take care of anyone you bring to my store, especially if you say they your boys."

As I looked around the jewelry store I spotted seven Rolex's just for me. I had to have me one "These right here, let me get three of these for now." I said pointing at the Rolex display case.

"You sure? I have better Rolex's than those. I have my Oyster Perpetuals and of course the Presidentials in the back." Tito replied trying to scam me out of more money. Little did he know his greed was only digging himself a deeper hole.

Trying to suppress my grin, I turned to him and said " Let's see what your working with then. Especially the Presidential" I had to pay special attention not to look at Peanut, knowing if I caught his eye one of us would laugh at this sucker, as we reeled him in.

While Tito gathered the watches together in the rear of the store I looked through the display case that the cash register sat on noticing some nice Fargo chains and some medallions that were off the hook. I knew once this transaction went through there would be no coming back to this store again for either me or Peanut. Everything was on my mind even a new wedding ring set for Brenda and I.

"Here are the watches I can give you a player deal on." said Tito when he came out of the back and presenting us with three of the most amazing Rolex's I'd ever seen before laying them on a

Enemies Amongst Us   D. Isaac

velvet cushion.

"I'll take them, all three." I said excited and anxious "There's three of us in our crew, and we'll probably need a fourth for our manager, but for now I like these, all three of them. The only problem being which one I want for myself" I said, adding a smile.

"How soon would you like them sir? Remember I have to get them cleaned up for you." Tito said using his best poker face to hide the excitement of such a sale.

"We're flying out tomorrow for the Soul Train awards and I can pick them up when we get back. I'll have to get the prices and have my manager bring you a check. That can happen today but I'm not in a rush I'd rather get them cleaned." I added nonchalantly

"Oh! No! You can wait as they get cleaned by the time you touch base with your manager and come back they'll be ready for you to wear out if that's what you desire." Tito says, trying not to let the money walk out the door. Every good salesman knows not to let the money walk out the door.

"Sounds good." I reply. "I'll give him a call right now." I add and start walking to the door to make my phony call to my phony manager.

"Listen, big man you came to the right place." Tito said, looking at Peanut sitting quietly in the corner reading a GQ magazine he'd found in a stack on a coffee table kept there for drivers and bodyguards of higher end customers.

After about five minutes on the phone with Marilyn outside, I walked back into the store thinking about what she was saying and was side tracked. We almost had to start everything over. My mind

Enemies Amongst Us   D. Isaac

was gone. She had just told me how happy she was with her new boyfriend and all of the sudden he didn't want to come home or explain why not. That angered me a little cause she was upset by it, and I didn't like anyone on my team being upset. I needed them at their best, at all times. I needed them to stay focused on the jobs at hand and that's exactly what I did as I walked back in the store my mind went straight back to getting the money that Tito was so graciously willing to give us.

When I entered I noticed that Peanut was by himself in the showroom "My bad where were we?" I asked taking off my Cartier frames and making eye contact for the first time.

"You good?" Asked Peanut, looking at my eyes

"Of course, everything is a go."

"Okay let me know something. You never take those cheap ass glasses off." Peanut jokes but also reminding me of my disguise.

"I'm good, I'm good." I replied placing the glasses back on my face. " My manager said we are leaving for a month maybe two on tour and I was only planning on two weeks." I said letting Peanut know I was back to normal.

"Word. Stay focused. He's in the back starting the cleaning process so we got a couple minutes to browse or whatever." Peanut said letting me know that Tito was moving on the sale.

The three tags were left on the counter from the watches. $24,000 , $21,000 and the cheapest being $14,000, was reserved for Peanut, as I would get the top tier ones for myself. One had a diamond bezel and diamonds all over the band with a black face. The other one had to have links added to fit my wrist but you couldn't deny it's value with blue face and same diamond bezel and band.

"What's the damage?" I asked Tito as he walked form the back drying his hands

Still running game and using his best poker face he replied " Only $59,000." doing his best to not only make it sound cheap but also hide his excitement "That's less than $20,000 each, and the high end ones are easily worth $30,000. Honestly a pawn shop would give you $14,000-$15,000 each and no one ever beats them out a dime." He finishes with a smile as he tosses the paper towel he was drying his hands with into a waste basket.

"Word. I had a budget of $100,000 so that's real good we will try and swing through tomorrow or I'll be back in a month or so when I get off tour. Maybe even send my manager I'm not sure yet." I said, still playing my part.

"Whatever works for you works for me. I'm your man in the diamond district remember that." he said kissing ass hoping to snag a return customer. "However I do got to ask what form of payment you'll be making."

"Pay him in cash, so I can get 30-40 bucks from him." Peanut jokes making it seem like he needed a cut out of the deal.

"Peanut," Tito says through a smile "You know I'll take care of you. I'll give you $41." he finishes with a laugh. Although it was more of an insult than as joke me and Peanut were quick to throw him a courtesy chuckle.

"I'm going to have my label cut you a check." I replied locking eyes with him before finishing "You don't expect me to walk

Enemies Amongst Us						D. Isaac

around with that kind of cash on me like a Drug dealer do you?"

"Absolutely not." he replied. "That would not be wise especially in this city. Now listen the total is $59,000. I'll cover the tax out of my pocket in hopes of snagging your future business. Just have your people cut that amount down into six different checks under $10,000 a piece and make sure to get them all certified. I'll polish the watches and have them shining and ready for you in the morning when you come."

He handed me a business card with the name to make the checks out to, and continued to bring up how big of a favor he was doing me by not charging me the sales tax. I left the store laughing to myself thinking this fools was protecting himself by asking for checks to be certified . What he really didn't know was who he was really fucking with. If I don't know you or don't care for you then I really don't care what happens to you. The whole world, especially Brooklyn, was a cherry pie and a real Goon is going to eat.

When I got back to Brooklyn, I went straight to Squeeze's spot. I told him the plan and that I needed six checks totaling $59,000. See Squeeze had this Italian connect that could certify the checks for a measly $500 a piece. A small price to pay as I was going to burn Tito for almost $60,000.

The next day at about 12 PM I pulled up to the front of Tito's place in my white Toyota Landcruiser, I parked it right in front despite the "no parking zone" sign, and left my truck running with the hazards lights blinking. I wanted Tito to see the truck there and think I couldn't leave it there to long without receiving a ticket or being towed. Thus giving me an excuse not to hang around while he gave the checks any extra attention.

Enemies Amongst Us   D. Isaac

    I told Peanut to watch the truck, went into the store, and handed Tito an envelope with the checks in it. He opened it and first thing checked to see they were certified. Then he added the totals and make sure they came to $59,000. After that he had the nerve to call the bank and double check the funds right in front of me. My heart sank as he explained what he was doing and picked up the phone dialing the number of the bank.

    I sprang to the offensive " Yo, Tito, these checks is good money. After all the bullshit you put me through, having my label write six different checks, just so you can dodge the IRS. Then getting them certified , now you got to call the bank?" I don't need this aggravation and honestly I don't have the time for it. I said with an attitude like I was insulted by him calling the bank to make sure my money was good.

    "And in case you don't remember I got a plane to catch and I don't need my fucking truck getting towed while you dick around in here. This ain't how you keep clients, just give me the checks back man I ain't fucking with you on this." I threatened.

    Hanging up the phone he pleaded "Wait, Wait, Jamal my bad man. You never know around here I've been scammed so many times. Your right, I'm sorry. I'll give you the checks back or the watches as we agreed. You pick."

    I pretended to think about this briefly then said "I'll take the watches and I want to do business with you, but you waste my time and insult me both of those need to be made right. So give me $2,500 off my next order." I said knowing damn well there wasn't going to be another order.

    He thought this over than replied "Of course big fella. Like I

Enemies Amongst Us   D. Isaac

said yesterday I'm your man in the diamond district ain't no need for you to go anywhere else." then handed me the a velvet cloth containing the watches.

"Good business, does good business." I said as we shook hands "I'll even tell all my buddies in the music biz about you and how you took care of me." Then turned towards the door before I started laughing. Sometimes I even amaze myself with the bullshit I come up with.

Once outside Peanut jumped back in the truck and we pulled out. On my way back to Brooklyn I gave him the plain gold Rolex, as we agreed for his fee for setting up Tito. I even asked him if he was worried about what Tito would do when he found out the checks were no good. He told me he wasn't and fuck Tito he was going back to Trinidad soon and would never see him again anyway. We both laughed as I dropped him off and we agreed that I would see him when I was down there for the carnival in February.

I then headed towards Squeezes house and broke him off with the black faced Rolex and kept the blue one for myself. Not bad for a couple hours work without using a gun. As the true saying goes "You gotta be in it to win". That was another one of my mottos.

About a month had passed and I hadn't thought about Tito once when my boy Paulie called me.

"Yo, Dread, what's good Son?"

"Ain't nothing Rudeboy." I replied.

"Yo, I just got off the phone with Haitian Jack and he told me that Spanish pussy ass mutha fucka, Tito, offered him a Rolly to find out who you was and shoot you."

"Say word?" I asked, with no real concern.

"Word to mother Son." Paulie laughed "You crazy Dread."

What Tito didn't know was Haitian Jack was my homeboy and wouldn't go against the grain. There is still a little honor amongst thieves.

Tito is the same jeweler that Haitian Jack took Tupac (RIP) to when he wanted to purchase jewelry similar to Jack's when they were still friends.

A lot of people in the entertainment industry, and hustlers still buy the pieces from Tito on 47th St. in the diamond district not knowing that he is really ripping them off by not giving them quality stones in the jewelry they purchase from him.

Chapter 15

Nothing was going to get in me and Squeeze's way of getting money, especially the minor threat from little bitches like Tito. He was nothing to me except a past jux. I came, I saw, I conquered and I went on to the next, simple as that.

Squeeze and I had a good thing going. His job was to print the checks and help find people to sell us credit cards along with recruiting people to go into the banks for us. I had the connections to make the fake ID's and get the information we needed to activate the credit cards. Also I knew a lot of females that were down to make some money. We each knew and played our role making us not only a good team but a good amount of money also.

One day squeeze said to me "Yo, Dread, I need you to get some ID's made up."

"I got it." I told him.

He gave me an envelope with some pictures and a list with names and information that he wanted on the ID's. We chopped it up for a while then I peeled off to go handle my end of the business.

Later on that day after I had gotten the ID's back from my African connect, I started looking through them closer to make sure all names and addresses matched up correctly with the profile of the check and credit cards. This is when I realized that one of the females on the ID was this fine ass red bone cutie that I had been checking out that worked down the block from my health food store. She was something to take home to mama and explain

Enemies Amongst Us   D. Isaac

why a slow, bitter divorce process was holding up your new marriage. I took that ID out of the envelope and put it in my pocket.

   Now this lady I hadn't formally met as of yet. I would just observe her in the mornings when she would walk past my store on her way to work. This young lady was about 5'9" with long black hair that reached the middle of her back. She had that bi-racial look about her, she could pass for Italian or Latina. She had a body like J-lo. Every time I'd seen her she was always dressed professionally in designer suits or dress shirts with slacks and shoes. Baby girl had a mean shoe game that turned me on. There was something exotic about her look and I knew from the first time I laid eyes on her that I needed her in my life.

   I had flirted with her a few times when she had come into my store to buy her vegetarian patties and carrot juice for her lunch when Brenda was not present. Even though I was married to Brenda at the time, I knew this woman was going to be in my life in the future. You see I had fallen for her from the very first sight of her.

   This is the part where some women would call me a dog, while some men would call me a playa, but as the good book says "Let he who is without sin cast the first stone."

   The next morning when I saw her, I called her over and said "Good morning Beautiful, how are you feeling this morning."

   "Just fine old man." she replied with a smile that could steal a soul.

   "Yeah you sure look fine baby girl." I answered taking my time as I looked her up and down letting her see me appreciate her from head to toe.

"What's that your wearing? A Donna Karen suit with Gucci shoes it sure looks good on you whatever it is." I said as I licked my lips.

She blushes and turns bright red In her cheeks and gave me that thousand watt smile, the one that could light up a whole Brooklyn block during a blackout.

Baby girl I need to have a serious conversation with you about something. I told her as I stared deep into her sexy brown eyes.

"Why don't you pick me up after I get off work at around five this evening. We could talk then."

"Okay beautiful I'm going to do that, but I'm going to need you to meet me around the corner form your job on Gates AVE." I said.

"Is this going to be okay with your wife?" she asked showing little concern.

"You don't worry about her I won't get you into anything I cant' get you out of Ma." I replied smoothly.

She just looked at me and gave me a smile and a conspiring wink before saying " I'll see you at 5 then. Don't be late." as she walked out the door.

I couldn't pick her up from the front of her job because Brenda would've seen me if she was looking out the window of our store, and I didn't want to deal with the fight her crazy ass would pick when I got home. So just like the group TLC sang in their hit song.

Enemies Amongst Us   D. Isaac

"I Creep" I had to keep my business with this woman on the super down low.

   I picked up baby girl after she had gotten off work and as soon as she got into my truck she asked "Can you take me to school while we talk?" Using those big brown eyes to make sure I said yes. Instantly I got hard as a rock and would've loved to lay the seat back and let her ride me right there on the spot, thinking nothing of who could possibly see. She was that sexy and had that effect on me.

   "Yeah, ma I can do that where you go to school at.?"

   "Out by Sheepshed Bay." She replied

   "So what is your name beautiful?" I finally asked her. "My name is Dee by the way some of my friends call me Dread."

   "My name is Brittney." she said, looking a little embarrassed that we had not exchanged names until now."Your name is as beautiful as you are. Brittney tell me a little about yourself? Were are you form? I hear a little accent out of you."

   "Well my father is Saudi and my mother is from Grenada, they met in England and that is where I was born."

   "You don't sound like and English person.

   "Well that's because I grew up over here in Texas." she replied

   "Really, you do sound a little country." I told her and she started laughing.

   So what are you doing way out here in the big apple?" I asked her.

"Well, I came up here to stay with my uncle he is going to pay for me to attend medical school as soon as I'm ready."

"That's what's up Ma, You got it going on then."

"You think so?"

"Hell yeah, I love a beautiful woman with a good head on her shoulders." I told her, flirting with her again making her blush.

"So what was so serious that you wanted to talk to me about?"

I showed her the ID with her face on it and I could tell that I had shocked the hell out of her by the expression on her face.

"How did you get that?" she exclaimed.

"From one of my partners that I do business with sometimes. The question is why is your face on here? And do you know what your getting yourself into?"

Brittney broke it down for me play by play on how one of her friends introduced her to Squeeze and told her that she could make some quick, easy money on the side by cashing a couple checks and shopping. After she had finished talking I went on to explain things to her.

"Do you know the risk and reward of your actions?" I asked.

"He said there isn't anyway, we couldn't get caught because he know what he is doing." she responded as naive as can be.

"Listen I want to let you know that you can create a criminal record by getting petty misdemeanors and build it to getting felonies. You will eventually accumulate both of them by cashing

Enemies Amongst Us
D. Isaac

checks and sliding cards. Nothing is guaranteed or promised. I would love to make the money off you and split it with my boy after you get a cut." keeping it real with her. I wanted this woman in my life and I had to put her up on game.

"I need the money. I'm trying to get out of my living situation and get my own place."

"Well there's a right and a wrong way to do things and if you can find other people who would do it I'll give you a cut so you can fix your living arrangement but I'm not letting you do it."

"Oh, so your my daddy now." she asked, dismayed.

"You know what Biggie say, "I love it when you call me Big Poppa." I said making her laugh real hard.

"Big Poppa huh?" she asked before I broke it all down to her on a serious note explaining what would happen further along. She had to go to school so I let her know I was going to shred everything with her factious name, and real photo on it. She came clean and told me she had a boyfriend, but she still wanted me to pick her up from school at 9 PM. I already knew that wasn't going to make out for the good of either of our relationships. I wanted to be her lover and I had three hours to properly prepare my proposal to them panties. I just didn't have an excuse or reason why I wasn't going to benefit financially from her. Squeeze wasn't going to be pleased with me putting paper before pussy. Sex was on my mind the entire time I was away form Brittney. I went to my stash house and showered up before putting on some nice clothes. I had my favorite tan Timbs on with my favorite black Tommy Hilfiger jean, and a solid tan polo button down. The Versace green jeans cologne I wore was going to get her without a doubt. I wasn't leaving no

Enemies Amongst Us   D. Isaac

room for dislike.

   The ride to the school seemed as if it took a lifetime or two. I played "Honey Love" by R Kelly it seemed like a hundred times. I was singing out loud and grooving the entire drive there. Once I arrived she was waiting patiently out front with a female companion just as beautiful as her.

  "After a long day of work and school you sure do disguise it well." I said complementing her beauty as she opened the door and sat in my Landcruiser.

  "Why you say that?" she replied as she straps on the seatbelt.

   "You look like your day barely started with your pretty self " I replied driving off. There was no way I could let her leave my presence without a tight hug and wet kiss. This lady was too fine, she had Brenda beat by a long shot and was years younger. A family and a future was on my mind..

  "Oh, wow, thank you I feel like crap my day has been long." she replied taking her hair out of a ponytail.

  "Is that how you like it?" I asked

  "Like what?" she asked innocent like.

  "Long." I replied

  "Yes, of course." she said catching on and looking out of the passenger window away from me on purpose.

  "How long?" I asked continuing to flirt.

  "Long enough to make me regret the moment." she said

looking at me so she could catch my reaction.

I shook my head and remained quiet to see what she would say next, and after a short silence I turned the music back on. She heard R. Kelly and her legs spread apart. I looked at her and she looked at me then we looked away briefly. Slowly we both turned to stare at each other again and it was on. There was no need for words.

I had a good time with Brittney and enjoyed her conversation. She was everything I expected and more. I learned that her uncle was taking care of her as she attended school, giving her money, paying her tuition and keeping a roof over her heard. All that was what I wanted to be doing. Brenda and I had a decent relationship that was over the second I met Brittney. I had to form an exit plan to get out of my marriage. Brenda was a cool 8 but I had me a young, fine go getter who was every bit of a dime piece. Everything about Brittney was pretty, sexy, and fine head to toe and back up. Not to mention she had a mean sex game.

During the first month of me getting my groove on with Brittney we incorporated a lot of time, having lots of sex. The sex was so good to us both, to the point we would go for hours like teenagers. She loved sucking and I loved fucking, so we did what we loved together. She had me, I had her and we were both well kept.

Creeping with Brittney wasn't a big problem being that my home girl Laverne form Trinidad, rented me her condo for $1,000 a month. The condo sat across the street from my store and down the street from Brittney's job, making it very convenient for us both. I was upset that Laverne had to leave her condo, but when a

Enemies Amongst Us   D. Isaac

woman has an abusive man I feel that's what all women should do. Move on and never look back. Whether it's verbal, emotional or physical, abuse is abuse.

    The condo became my stash spot where my boy Pat would live full time. My wife Brenda knew nothing about what wasn't her business so there was nothing to tell her about my stash house. I had the most peaceful moments at that stash house just like the ones in the past. I should of called them my get away cribs even though they were always so close. The feeling was like I was on vacation any time I walked through the doors.

    After laying up with Brittney for three or four months she called me and said " Yo Dee, I'm pregnant." Before I could reply she broke down crying. I wasn't sure what had happened or why she was crying so I just listened for a minute. Then when I tried to talk I realized I was speechless. It was as if a cat had my tongue. It takes courage to stand up and speak and courage to sit down and listen, understanding that I started to speak.

    "Congratulations my dear." I spoke with good punctuation and a clear intriging tongue.

    "Your not mad?" she asked worried about what my wife would think or how I'd react.

    "No! Not by far, this is the best day of my life." I responded, then added "I got you babe we are going to be alright." Contemplating my next move without a clue of what I was going to do. Analyzing the situation there I was married, cheating, in love on the side of my adultery, and now with a child on the way. If my wife would've gotten pregnant within the last two year prior I wouldn't even be in such a situation. I'm a man though so I handled it like I was suppose to and just played the cards that was dealt to me.

    Not long after, maybe a day or two later Brittney uncle found the pregnancy test she had used and told her if she was old enough to have sex she was grown enough to live on her own. He put her out in New York knowing she's from Texas like he was in a relationship with her. I mean it's one thing she's pregnant and she needs to raise her own child, but the child wasn't born and she was already kicked to the curb. The uncle didn't care if she had somewhere to go or not he just told her to beat feet. Luckily I had my stash spot and a little money on the side. Not only did he tell her to get out but cut her tuition and any help at all.

    The news Brittney delivered wasn't the best of news, but in a way it wasn't bad either. I left the store, went to the condo, grabbed Pat and we went and helped her get her things. When I called Pat he thought I had beef with someone in the streets considering I told him "We got to roll, I need you to help me with something I'm downstairs right now."

    "Bring the little ones, or the little and big ones?" He asked trying to figure out what guns to grab before he came downstairs.

    "Nothing like that, Britt's pregnant and her uncle just kicked her out of his house. She's packing her stuff and we're going to go get her."

    "Say no more." he replied ending the call and picking up two handguns just in case her uncle got sporty at the mouth.

    Once Pat jumped in the ride he started asking me questions about family. I didn't know where he was going with the conversation, he was just yapping.

"Aye, Dee, you mean to tell me family would just put you out because they don't approve of you being grown and doing what grown folks do. I'm saying he just put her out like she have somewhere to go. I'm sure if she had somewhere to go she wouldn't have been living with him. Then she is in school, trying to better herself, and he's just going to say fuck her. That shits dirty Son."

"Man it's all good, I'll take care of my woman and my child we don't need him, real talk."

"I know you don't my man, but still family is family and that shit is fucked up."

"It's all to the good. He thinks he hurt her but it's only going to make her stronger." I said, reaching over for a dap.

"Oh your going to wife her now? I know you been wanting another seed since you came home."

"Right and now I got another on the way. I'm happy now. The only problem is how long can I keep this off Brenda's radar?"

"You'll figure it out Big Dogg. If anyone know you it's me, and I'm sure you got this under control.

I moved Brittney into the condo that Laverne was renting me and after a few days Pat moved in with his brother. He wasn't happy about the outcome but he was truly understanding. I couldn't have him laying around my girl while I was with my wife it wouldn't have been a good look at all. With Brittney expecting a child I had to be the only influence in her ear after her uncle pulled his shit.

Chapter 16

Weeks after Brittney was comfortable and loving her new place. I received a phone call from one of the other girls I'd been messing around with. This wasn't just any old fling, Nikkia was one of them girls any straight man would love to call his friend. She was funny, out going, sensitive and tenacious in every setting. I took her more of a Toni Braxton but some say she had more of a Mary J. Blige glow about her. She was all around fine and good like a well seasoned wine, just the sound of her voice on the phone could lift my spirits and warm my body.

One day when I'm cruising around Brooklyn she hit me on my cell "Hey, Big Daddy, what're you doing?" she asked when I answered.

"Just chilling, checking some traps lil mama. How bout you?"

"I'm just wonderful, chillin at my crib."

"What's on your agenda today?" I asked, hoping that I was.

"I got something I need to holler at you about, can you swing by for a little bit?"

"Absolutely, I'll be there in a couple minutes just let me pull up on my boy and drop him some work and I'll be right there." I replied not wanting her to know that I was really just on the prowl for a lick, or a chick, or both.

When I pulled up in front of Nikkia's house she was standing out front waiting on me looking real sexy in a short jean Guess skirt, that showed a lot of legs, and a tight t-shirt showing off her ample cleavage. She stood on her stoop waiting for me to get out of my SUV before she made her move towards me.

"You can get back in the truck." she said, as I came within a couple steps of her. I wanted a hug maybe a kiss, not to be shut down and turned around. I was going to squeeze her fat ass real tight, but even that went out the window when she demanded I get back into my truck.

Once she was seated in my truck she said, "Dee, I'm pregnant." slapping me across the face with those three words. I was not ready to hear that again so soon especially from another female. I'd rather she told me she needed money to go shopping and its no secret how much I love my money, but not another baby. No! No! this couldn't be happening to me. Not one after another. I just sat there in a daze for a few seconds feeling a confused mix of happy, and scared. Not knowing what to do or say my brain locked up and I just spoke.

"What?"

"I said I'm pregnant Dee." she repeated.

"Girl stop playing with me." I told her not wanting to believe my ears.

"I'm not playing with you Dee I'm ready to spend the rest of my life with you now. What are we gonna do? You do love me right?" She said, dead serious.

"Yeah baby, you know I love you girl."

Enemies Amongst Us   D. Isaac

"Then what are we gonna do fool?" she asked, laughing as I sat there staring out the front window, dazed, trying to let the news soak in to my already overwhelmed brain.

"Huh?" I replied coming back to reality.

"What are we gonna do about this baby?" she asked, hitting me on the shoulder with a love tap.

"What do you mean what are we gonna do?" I asked, the added " What do you want to do?"

"I'm ready for you to leave your wife so we can start a family. I'm willing to give you all of me if your willing to give me all of you, so we can start a family. You said I make you happy and your wife Brenda don't so marry me and let's build this family. Let's let this baby be the start." she said looking at the complete shock that must be written all over my face.

"Say something if you want me to have this baby because I'm not gonna be just another baby mama struggling to make ends meat cause my baby daddy got caught up in the streets. Dee I don't want to live my life as someone's side chick while you live with another woman. Look at me I can have any man but I chose you, I love you Dee." she carried on.

"Damn, Baby your serious?" I finally replied trying to figure out how I had gotten myself into this situation in the first place.

"Yes, I'm serious as cancer, diabetes, aids and a gunshot."

I realized I couldn't' talk this one out with my wife, my love, best friend, life partner, Brenda. I was actually even getting mad at Brenda for not being able to have children. I been consistently

Enemies Amongst Us   D. Isaac

laying wood to her and busting good nuts trying to get her pregnant and it wasn't happening. I guess it wasn't Gods will.

"What do you want to do? I'm team us, I just don't know right now I need some time to think, I do love you so don't get that misunderstood." I explained, then finished "I just need a little time to think."

"Your right! Your right." she said, with a attitude as she opened the door to exit my SUV. "You are damn right and I'm seriously gonna give you some time to think about what you want to do." she said as she slammed the door and all that beautiful ass walked away.

Just three days after my conversation with Nikkia, I'm driving down Linden Blvd, in Flatbush, on my way to Squeeze's crib to put some money together when my phone started ringing. I dropped it as I tried to answer while I was driving. I shoulda taken the hint my phone was trying to tell me I wasn't ready for this phone call at this point in my life.

"What's up Papi?" What are you doing? It sound like you talking and driving, you know that ain't safe." Jennifer says in greeting. Jennifer is a fine ass Panamian chick I been digging in for the last year or so.

"Oh, I'm not up to nothing Mami? Just missing your sexy ass." I responded flirting around.

"You are to much. I have some good news for you Papi." she said, full of excitement then added "Guess what Papi?"

"Just tell me girl, you know I ain't no good at guessing games. Just tell me what's up babe and quit teasing me, you know if you

Enemies Amongst Us									D. Isaac

get this big boy up and going your gonna have to deal with him." I said hoping she'd tell me about something sexy she was wearing.

"Your gonna be a father, I'm gonna be a mother, and we're gonna buy a big mansion and live happily ever after." she exclaimed.

"What? You lost me babe." I responded, hoping she wouldn't repeat herself. Denial is a beautiful thing.

"I'm pregnant Papi." she shouted loudly, her voice filled with joy and excitement. I almost crashed my fucking truck when I heard those words come out of her mouth. I didn't know what was worse, it seems all I heard anymore was "I love you Dee. I'm pregnant Dee. I'm pregnant Papi."

"Hold on babe let me pull over and let this register please. I said steering off to the right side of the road. I couldn't believe what had happened to me I felt dumbfounded.

In all actuality Brenda was the victim but I felt like I was the one in grave danger. Three beautiful women who loved me and that I could happily spend the rest of my life with were all pregnant at the same time. I wanted to feel like a stud playa but death was hanging out with me and I felt it. It has been hard living with Brenda knowing Brittney and Nikkia were pregnant and now Jenifer too? This wasn't healthy in any way. I knew one thing for sure and that was I wanted all three of the babies but I didn't know how I was gonna keep them a secret from my wife. Little did I know it would only be a matter of time before she found out anyway.

After I had calmed down form the initial shock, I said to

Enemies Amongst Us   D. Isaac

Jennifer "I'm gonna come over to your house so we can talk as soon as I'm finished handling this business."

"Okay, Papi I will see you when you get here, go make that money Mami need some new shoes, clothes, diapers, and wipes." she said ending the call and thinking she was funny.

When I got to Squeeze's house I fell on too the couch face down, to stressed to want to look at the world.

"Yo, Dread you alright?" He asked still standing in the doorway after letting me in.

"Yeah, man." I strung my words out "I'm just a little fucked up in the head right now that's all." I continues as I turned my face towards the door.

"What's going on? What's with you? Wanna talk?" He asked questioning me three times ignoring the fact that I had ignored the first one, then the second, and still had nothing to say to the third.

"Man." I finally broke weak then added "3 of 4 girls I'm fucking are pregnant and they all told me within the last month." I confided in him.

"Oh shit, your wife and who else? Man you sure have done it this time." he said shaking his head.

"Not my wife. Fuck I wouldn't feel so bad if it was."

"Not your wife? Then who? Nikkia, Brittney, and that fine Panamanian chick?"

"Yes them, isn't that some weird shit? I've been trying to get Brenda pregnant for two whole years and all I've received is failure. You know I had to start a family." I said sitting up on the sofa.

"So what're you gonna do?"

"I'm not sure yet, but I do want all my babies. I'm just going to have to step my hustle game up and make some money to take care of all of them. My father didn't do shit for me since I was born, and I refuse to be another dead beat daddy like him, feel me?"

"Yeah, I feel you on that one. Whatever you decide to do just know that I'm here for you if you need me. By the way I need to get the information to activate those credit cards on the table." He said giving me work to do since I would be needing more money to take care of my stable of new mothers and tribe of new children.

"Alright I got you, I'm gonna swing by my girl Marilyn's real estate office and run the credit reports after I go talk with Jennifer and bring the info for you first thing tomorrow." I said, as I picked up the cards and headed for the door.

When I pulled up to Jenifer's house her mother stood with her by the front door as I walked up. They both were smiling ear to ear as if they'd planned this pregnancy. I remember Jenifer telling me before how she over heard her mother talking on the phone with one of her coworkers at Kings County Hospital in Flatbush. I didn't pay no mind at all, Jessica was an only child so I knew our baby would be extra spoiled. Her mother loved children and the private house they lived at in Canarsie could become a good hide out for me.

"Hey mami how are you?" I greeted Jenifer's mom as I stepped in for a hug.

"I'm doing real good son how are you?" she replied, stepping away after the embrace.

"I can't complain, I'm excited and nervous to say the least. I guess you know already, your daughter is sharing a blessing form God with me." I spoke smiling at Jenifer as she grabbed my hand and led us through the front door of their home.

"Come in Papi you looking so nervous rather than your usual arrogant self." Jenifer says with a smile.

"I'm good babe don't trip." I reply as she led me to the sofa in the living room.

"You want something to drink?"

"Yes please, something cold please. You caught me off guard with the news earlier, it felt like someone, I don't know, punched me in the face and knocked me out before they took off running."

"You'll be okay it's going to be alight Dee you don't have to be scared I'm the one who will have all the aches, pains, and swelling, not you." she replied.

"What did your mother say?" I asked then added " But before you answer that I want you to know I'm not gonna miss one doctor visit with you."

"I would love that, my mother would feel the same. Before you pulled up she was talking about that. She said for me to be happy and for you to be around is very important for the baby." She replied as her mother interrupted.

"You two I will be back shortly I have to go pick up dinner.

Enemies Amongst Us   D. Isaac

The pregnant girl wants to eat pizza tonight." as she headed out the door.

"Okay." Jessica yelled to her back.

"Be here when I get back Dee." her mom ordered before closing the door behind her.

"Yes, Ma'am." I replied to the shut door. I was under the assumption she was telling me not asking me.

With her mother gone we picked up our conversation.

"You know you caught me off guard with this news, don't you."

"It's gonna be all good Dee. Don't trip my mother wants me to have the baby, she wants a grandchild."

"Yeah?" I asked.

"Yes Papi I got you, you should be happy now let me help you relax." she said leaning over and sticking her tongue in my mouth kissing me hungrily.

"Ohh yeah, that's better." she moaned into my ear as she felt my manhood responding to her aggression.

Jennifer was about 5'4" with long wavy hair that reached down the middle of her back. She had a rosy red complexion like an Indian, a pair of perfect mouth full size breasts, and nice round squeezable ass the size of two volley balls. She had a strong resemblance to the model/video vixen Ayisha Diaz. As we continued to kiss on the couch Jen started fumbling with the zipper of my pants. Once she had found what she was looking for she started stroking me with her soft hands.

Enemies Amongst Us   D. Isaac

"Baby stop." I pleaded "What if your mom comes home and catches us right here?"

"She ain't coming back Papi plus she already knows that I'm already pregnant and that your the father, so relax I got this." she said, as she straddled my lap and let the straps of her dress fall off her shoulders exposing her beautiful breasts.

I didn't need anymore encouragement after that. I palmed both her ass cheeks and started massaging them as I sucked first one nipple then the other making sure they both got the attention they deserved.

As I massaged her cheeks I noticed she wasn't wearing any panties and had to ask "Where is your panties at girl?" stopping what I was doing just to raise her frustration.

She looked at me like I was crazy and just smiled at me and said "When you told me you were coming over I took them off cause I knew you was gonna give me some when you got here."

"Oh yeah?" I asked then added "And what if I say no, you can't have none?"

"Papi you know what they say about us Panamanian ladies having that while liver." she said, as she reached between her legs, grabbed my penis, slid it into her soaking wet opening and started riding me like she was at a rodeo.

"Just relax and enjoy me Papi." she moaned as I met her thrust for thrust until sweat beaded on her forehead and between her breasts. As I watched her breathing become faster and faster as she moved closer to climax. "Just a few more....Aye...Aye Papi.... Aye Papi that's it give it to me." she begged.

Enemies Amongst Us
D. Isaac

Her moans filled my ears and I knew she was close. I was determined not to pull out so I grabbed her butt cheeks and stood up, laying her down on the carpet and putting a leg over each shoulder so I could enforce my will on her.

"Yes Papi,......Yes Papi..... Aye Dee... Aye Papi..... ohhh yeah...ohh yea that's it Papi give it to me, stroke this pussy." she begged as I long stroked her into orgasm.

"Who's pussy is this?" I asked, pulling out before drilling back into her.

"Yours Papi.... It's yours." she moaned.

"Who's pussy is this?" I repeated stopping mid-stroke like I was gonna take it out.

"It's your pussy Dee" she cried as she grabbed my ass and pulled me deep in to her up turned hips. "I'm cumming Dee,.........ohhh I'm cumming baby... ahh yesss....yess ahhhh." she moaned out as we came together.

I collapsed on her and we lay there for a few minutes as my heart beat hammered against her as she did her best to catch her breath, struggling more than normal under my full weight.

"I love you Papi." she said as she regained her breath and locked eyes with me.

"I love you to Mami." I replied returning her stare.

"Now when are you gonna leave that bitch so we can start being a family?" she asked, fucking up the whole after sex vibe with her seriousness.

Enemies Amongst Us   D. Isaac

"Damn Ma! Where did that come from all the sudden?" I asked, not ready to have this conversation.

"Dee, if you want me and this baby in your life, you got to put us first. I'm not gonna be second or put up with only seeing you during the daytime. I need a full time man and my baby is gonna need a full time dad. I watched my mother go through that bullshit with my father and I'm not gonna go through the same thing with you."

"Damn baby where is all this coming from?"

"Listen Dee." she said letting me know she was serious, every time she called me Dee I knew she meant business, the rest of the time I was Papi. "I want you to take some time and think about what I said so you can get your priorities straight then let me know what you want to do."

"Okay Ma." I replied reaching over to rub her tits.

"No Dee, that's it, I'm not playing with you I'm dead serious." she said, as she started fixing up her clothes.

"Alright Ma, you know I'm gonna handle my responsibilities." I said, getting my pants back on then adding "Let me digest everything you have said and come up with a plan that will make us happy."

Neither one of us wanting to jump the gun or argue we said our goodbye's and she gave me a juicy kiss and pushed me out the door so I could take some personal time and contemplate the jam I found myself in.

Chapter 17

About two weeks after my conversation with Jennifer, I decided to confront Brenda about why she hadn't been able to get pregnant.

On Thursday night after a nice hot bubble bath with my wife. Thoughts of Jennifer, Nikkia and Brittney all came to my mind. It was about two week after my last conversation with Jennifer about her pregnancy. We had some amazing sex in the bathtub, on the sink, and on the bed. We even had a quick round on the floor. My conscious didn't bother me until we laid in bed rejuvenating and watching TV. I didn't want to spoil the night but I need the answers. I knew at that point I wasn't the problem and to seek for a solution.

As we lay there, her head on my chest, and watched "Boomerang" with Eddie Murphy and Halle Berry. I asked her, "What's up my love?"

"Ain't nothing, I was just thinking about Halle Berry she my favorite actress. What's up with you? do you want something to drink." she asked.

"No I'm good, I was just wondering why you haven't blessed me with a beautiful son or daughter yet. As long as we been trying it seems like you can't get pregnant. Why do you think you haven't gotten pregnant yet"? I asked.

"Why do we have to talk about this tonight after we just made sweet love and are trying to relax? Do you just want to argue?" she asked, as she raised her head off my chest and sat with her back towards the headboard.

Enemies Amongst Us   D. Isaac

"You mad?" I asked turning her face towards me then repeating myself "You mad Brenda?"

"I'm just saying why are you trippin'" she snapped, as she threw the covers over me and stood up.

"If you walk out of this room I'm walking out if this house Brenda, I need you to talk to me right now. You ain't sneaking birth control on me is you?"

"Hell no! I ain't using no damn birth control." she said, getting all indignant with me looking down at me as she stood next to the bed.

"Then why the fuck you haven't gotten pregnant yet? I have been home for over two years giving you this good dick and your ass still ain't got pregnant yet." I said, my anger rising from her coping an attitude.

"Sit down let me talk to you we are husband and wife not fuck buddies." I demanded letting my anger show.

"Maybe there is something wrong with you." she said holding her ground and continuing to stand as tears started to roll down her face.

"What?" I asked.

"Maybe your shooting blanks or something. Why don't you go see a doctor?" she asked

I couldn't believe my ears and what I was hearing from her. Was she crazy? I just looked at her stunned and speechless thinking if she knew that I currently had three buns in the oven she'd probably

Enemies Amongst Us   D. Isaac

have a heart attack. I couldn't tell her that because her crazy ass would've probably tried to stab me while I slept. So like any other man would do I just kept my thoughts to myself and asked her "Why don't we both do that?" Let's set up a doctors appointment and get checked out together as married couple."

"Alright." she conceded, then laid back down in bed with me.

As time went by I kept telling Brenda to make an appointment so we could go to the doctor to get checked out, but all she did was make excuse after excuse. I started to resent her because I knew she was lying to me about something. I knew there was nothing wrong with me, I knew I wasn't shooting blanks.

I had married Brenda while I was in prison. She was there for me when nobody else was, when I really needed someone to hold me down. She was a good wife to me and I believed in my heart that she truly loved me for me. I also realized that I loved her but I was no longer in love with her. That being said I knew I couldn't just up and leave her after all she had sacrificed for me.

When I told Nikkia and Jenifer that I was not leaving my wife they both were furious. The both told me that they had to do what was best for them and the babies. Nikkia moved in with some dude and stopped talking to me for a while. Jennifer started avoiding me all together. Brittney was the coolest about the situation and never put any pressure on me to leave my wife, she acted as if she was content enough just having me in her life.

When Brittney was about three months into her pregnancy I had spent the night with her at the condo. Brenda was supposed to be in Long Island, spending time with her family. About 7 AM I hear the alarm on my truck going off outside. I shot out of bed and looked out the window, not seeing anything wrong with my truck I turned off the alarm with the remote on my keychain and went back to bed.

Brittney was in the bathroom drying her hair and getting ready for work. After she had finished getting dressed and was about to leave I took my turn in the bathroom. While I was in there she yelled at me "baby I'm gonna take the trash out for you." as she was on her way out the door.

"Okay Sweet-cheeks enjoy your day." I yelled, as I relieved myself.

Next thing I know there is a ruckus coming from the living room as the television is knocked from he stand and crashes onto the floor. I hear screaming and the undeniable sounds of a scuffle and I automatically think that it's the feds raiding me or some stick up kid trying to make a quick lick out of me. I'm stuck... brain frozen for a minute. I'm in the middle of one of those long early morning pisses that never seem to end. When I finally finish and run into the living room, I find Brenda has Brittney pinned on the couch and is raining blows on her.

Brenda was screaming and she is saying "I told you he was my husband." over and over as she poured both tears and fists upon Brittney.

I rushed over and pulled Brenda off her. When I looked down Brittney's white blouse was covered in blood. My mind automatically clicked to the worst thinking she lost the baby. Looking at all the blood all I could think was Brenda killed my baby I turned to her and screamed.

Enemies Amongst Us   D. Isaac

"What the fuck do you think your doing?"

"She knew we were married." she yelled back venom in her voice.

"What?"

"That bitch be coming into the store talking to me when your not around and I told her we were married."

Dumb founded by the news I let the shock run through me. The whole time Brittney had been coming to peep game from Brenda behind my back. Some women could be trifling.

"Get her the fuck out of here Dee." Brittney screamed then added "Get her the fuck out of my house." before stomping off to the bathroom to clean herself up.

I watched her go still in shock before Brenda yelled "You gonna let that bitch tell you what to do huh?" breaking my trance.

Back in reality, I had to stop this madness before the neighbors called the cops, so I grabbed Brenda by the arm and led her to the door

"Come on Brenda you got to, wait outside while I put some clothes on I'll be out in a minute." I said, as I opened the door for her and nudged her out of it.

After I had gotten Brenda in the hallway and locked the door, I went back to check on Brittney in the bathroom.

"You alright baby girl?" I asked, my concern obvious.

"Yeah, that bitch sucker punched me when I opened the door

right in the fucking nose."

"How's your stomach?" I was worried about her loosing the baby especially with all the blood I'd seen on her blouse.

"It's alright, I think. She didn't hit me there."

"Listen I'm gonna run outside and talk to her and try to straighten this shit out and get her away from here. I'll be back as soon as I can." I explained, as she went to get dressed and I went to deal with Brenda.

When I came outside Brenda was waiting for me "What the fuck took you so long? Had to make sure your bitch was alright?" she screamed getting up in my face.

Brenda was only about 5'5" and 120 pounds but I had to give it to her she was 100 percent heart. She must of sense something in my demeanor because she quickly backed up and said " Come on and hit me. just come on and hit me for that slut. and I'm gonna lock your ass up nigga." she yelled as the tears streamed from her eyes.

I just looked at her not believing my ears knowing she knew about how I felt about the police. It saddened me to see what we'd become. I could never be with a woman that threatened to bring the law into our affairs and she knew it. That was my main rule when dealing with women and Brenda had just threatened to violate it.

"I ain't gonna hit you Brenda, go on home and I'll see you when I get there." I commanded

"I ain't going home, I'm moving back to my parents house and

Enemies Amongst Us   D. Isaac

you can stay here with your fake white bitch." she said as she walked off, got into her mothers car and drove off.

After she had driven off I jumped up in the air full of joy. She thought she was hurting me by leaving me, and in a way it did. However, overall she was doing me a favor instead. Now I didn't have to come up with an excuse to leave her.

By the time I got back upstairs Brittney had changed her clothes and cleaned up. She was now ready to go to work and I was free to walk her there hand in hand. No more sneaking around worrying about Brenda catching me anymore. Sometimes blessings are in disguise.

After about two months after Brenda left I found myself missing her a lot. Even though I was happy to be with Brittney, I still had a special connection with my wife. I couldn't just let my love go without making amends to her heart for all my selfishness. Her parents loved her being back home with them in Long Island. I just couldn't call her because of my guilt, luckily I didn't have to cause she made that move for me.

"What's up Dee? How've you been?" she asked, as I answered my phone.

"Hello Brenda, I'm fine how about yourself?" I replied, surprised to hear her voice.

"I miss you Dee."

"I miss you to girl and you know the store isn't the same without you I really could use you around here. I'm so so apologetic for my actions. I never meant to cause you such pain. You married me when I was in prison and all alone. You were there

Enemies Amongst Us   D. Isaac

for me when no one else was. When I really needed someone to hold me down I had you. You've been a very good wife and I know you truly do love me. It saddens me that I don't know how to show you the same love in return. You've sacrificed so much for me and invested tons." I cried out giving her closure to my madness that caused all her hurt.

" I accept you apology Dee and I thank you for understanding who I have been in your life." she replied calmly then continued " I miss you more Dee, trust me. Can you come see me after you close the store tonight?" she asked.

"Yeah, I suppose. I can do that."

I will be here bring me something to eat and a couple hundred dollars please."

"Okay I will see you when I close the store." I replied ending the call. Little did I know Brenda had been parked across the street from the store watching me form her friends car all day.

As I locked up the store to go to Brenda's parents, I noticed I had forgot to set the alarm on the store. I doubled back after driving for five minutes and I noticed the same car that had been parked across the street all day was pulling out as I parked behind it. I paid it no mind only focusing on reuniting with my wife as I ran in and set the alarm.

Arriving at Brenda's parents, I was greeted by her mother who explained that Brenda had just called and was only a couple minutes away. She offered me a meal and something to drink as she began small talk. " How's the store? How long do you plan to stay separated?" Etc.. I really didn't wanna answer all these

Enemies Amongst Us   D. Isaac

questions but I knew if I was to going to seek forgiveness from Brenda having her mom on my side was crucial.

   Thirty minutes after I'd gotten to her parent's Brenda walked through the door jolly and filled with joy. I knew it couldn't of been because I was present. Had that been the case she would've been there when I got there. She'd been in my life long enough to know what time I closed the store and exactly how long it would take me to get to her parents house. Again I didn't think anything of it, my wife was in my presence and the only thing on my mind was repentance.

  Brenda and I sat and talked about our differences and my need for a child. She cried and lied blaming me for her not being happy. Never did she understand what I was saying or trying to say when she would cut me off. Finally my phone rang interrupting our conversation

  "Yo Dread, your store is on fire where you at?" My childhood friend Stephen yelled through the phone.

  "What?" I asked in shock.

  "The health food store is burning down." he replied even louder, then added "I'm standing in front of your store watching it go down in blazes homie."

  "Man stop playing, I just left there an hour ago." I said, hoping he was just kidding. "Dread I ain't playing homie. I'm standing right here in front of your spot and it is defiantly on fire. You hear that noise ? That's a fire truck you hear in the background coming to put out the fire right now. Yo Rick, come here and tell Dread what's going on he thinks I'm playing with him." He finishes, passing his phone to my other homie Rick.

"Yo Dread, its all bad he ain't playing, your store is burning down for real."

"All right, alright I'll be there in 45 minutes." I told them before hanging. I dropped everything and left without speaking to Brenda or her mother. Brenda was looking at me kind of funny. I didn't think anything of it until I got halfway back to Brooklyn.

My mind raced the entire drive back to my store. Rick or Stephen never mentioned my windows were broken so the fire had to of happened inside the store. Brenda had the only extra set of keys and had lured me all the way out to Long Island while she had someone go in the store and started the fire. She must of felt that since our relationship was over she would hurt me by burning the store down. She wasn't having no other woman share what she helped build.

When I arrived at the store and seen the damage I knew it was hopeless. I didn't have insurance and the store was a loss to rebuild. I drove away after a few minutes and just licked my wounds. It didn't matter who or what, it was all over, another chapter of my life finished. Back to the hustle, back to the grind.

Like any natural born hustler I went back to the streets full time. I wasn't gonna let yesterdays loss effect today's win. We don't cry over spilt milk in Brooklyn. We are known for taking money or dying trying.

Chapter 18

Enemies Amongst Us   D. Isaac

Brenda didn't hurt me by burning down our health food store, she actually helped me in a sense. I was now able to do me and be myself again. It felt good getting back to the hustle with no obligations to fulfill or excessive bills to pay. If it was up to me I would've invested the money I put into the health food store into a night club or a decent sports bar. We live and we learn to recognize all obstacles for what they are. Obstacles.

Back in the streets doing whatever to make ends meet, I found myself selling cellular phone and paying the bills with stolen profiles and credit cards. When cell phones first came on the scene the bill to maintain one was very expensive. All the hustlers wanted them because they were the newest gadget out and it made life much more convenient. A young entrepreneur from the ghetto of Bedford-Styvesant, Brooklyn by the name of Gordon came up with a way to clone the cell phones and save everybody in the hood a whole lot of money while making himself a small fortune in the process.

I had bought this electronic chip that I could attach to the bottom of the Erickson Cellular phones and activate them by entering what is called the ESN numbers along with the connecting phone number in about three minutes. I had bought this little gadget from a friend of mine by the name of Jay, who happened to be a member of Gordon's crew. Jay would also sell me sheets of ESN numbers along with corresponding phone numbers whenever I'd need them.

In order to get the ESN numbers along with the phone numbers, Gordon had a machine that was called a scanner and he would set up this machine in a room close to a highway, and aim it out the window at cars driving by. The machine would snatch the signal from anybody driving by using a cellular phone then print out the ESN and phone numbers. This simple method would allow us to clone the new cell phones that we would buy and use somebody else's phone number to talk while they paid the bill for it.

    This quickly became another of my side hustles as I was still handling business with Squeeze as well. When out shopping with the credit cards, I would tell everybody to but me cell phones and computers. It was nothing for me to be riding around in my truck with about 30-50 new cell phones. During the week I would drive around the city all day selling phones to other hustlers for $200 each. When their phones got turned off I'd turn them back on for another $100 extending them for an additional month of service. Word started spreading about cell phone service for a hundred dollars a month and people could talk as much as they wanted on them. Everybody in New York wanted one and like the saying goes "Monkey see, monkey do," A lot of other people started getting in on the cloning phone hustle.

    When I couldn't get Jay to supply me with numbers, I started using the information from the credit card reports that I would use to activate the cards Squeeze and I were running. This process was just as easy. All I had to do was call up the phone company and tell them that I had just purchased a cell phone and I wanted to activate it. They would ask me my name, social security number, and date of birth. I would recite the information into the phone like I was the actual person then when they asked for a billing address, I would tell them to send it to a bogus business address. I had a few girls just sitting around their houses doing this for me all day sometimes.

Enemies Amongst Us
D. Isaac

One day while I was cruising down Nostrand Ave in Crown heights, Brooklyn. I saw one of my Jamaican buddies from back in the days, Mugsy. He and I grew up together and he used to live in the Vanderveer housing projects in the early eighties. He was standing on the corner of Park Place in front of Surf's Record Store. Surf was another friend of mine who was also born in Jamaica, but migrated to America to make a better life for himself and his family.

I pulled over in front of the record store so I could kick it with Mugsy for a minute since I hadn't seen him in a while.

"What ah gwan rude boy?" I greeted him as he climbed into the Dodge Caravan I was driving.

"Nothing nah gwan Dex." He replied in his thick Jamaican accent ." I just got back into the country from being deported and I'm broke. I need some help Dex. What's up? Beg yah something nah man?" He pleaded.

"I got you Rude Boy don't worry." I said, peeling off a hundred dollars, from the knot I had stuffed in my pocket , handing it and a call phone to him.

"Starr, what yah doing with all dem phones inna yah car? Put me down with you I need to make some money." He said.

"Mugs this is slow money, it ain't like when we used to sell drugs and rob Colombians and Dominicans back in the eighties and nineties."

"I don't care I don't got nothing going on. You know I got five kids and my wife, Sheryl, to support."

Enemies Amongst Us   D. Isaac

"Alright Rude Boy this is what we are going to do, I'm going to start giving you credit cards and fake ID's to go along with them, all you got to do is go into stores and buy computers, phones, and all types of electronics that we can sell, and I will split the money with you 50/50 after I take out what the cards cost me." I explained.

"That's it?"

"That and whenever I get a call for a jux, we go and smash it."

"Bet starr, I'm down with you." he replied shaking my hand.

"A'right rude boy I'ma give you a call tomorrow so we can hang out and I'll show you the ropes."

"Do that brethren and don't front on me. I'ma look for your call." He said, as he exited the van.

****

My family life was going to be beginning soon and with a healthy savings and decent checking account I knew Brittney and I had plenty. She wasn't the material type of girl but she did like nice things. A little Gucci here and a little Prada there wouldn't hurt her and the baby that was coming soon. I think Brittney enjoyed being pregnant more than she did before. I gave her plenty of attention and we spent a lot of time together. By 8PM I was home every night. I would not leave the house until 9AM most mornings just to make sure she got the quality time she needed. Maternity leave had come early for her, due to aches and pains she was having after Brenda attacked her like a rab id pit-bull. I loved coming home to Brittney much more than I did Brenda. I felt like I had something to look forward to with Brittney. She felt like a soul mate. I knew

Enemies Amongst Us   D. Isaac

in my heart she was born to be mine.

"Hey Babe, how was your day?" she asked as I opened the door to our home.

"This is actually the best part of my day. I work, hustle, grind or whatever you want to call it just for you and everything you produce. I love you Brit. " I replied, hugging and kissing her as she sat on the sofa and did her crossword puzzle.

"What did you do today?" she asked, genuinely curious.

"I loved and missed you." i replied, then added "What'd you do today?"

"I loved and l missed you all day...waiting for you to walk through the door and make me really appreciate the day." she stated with a smile before kissing my lips.

"I bumped in to my old friend Mugsy in front of Surf's and I made us a little money. Here put this up to go to the bank tomorrow and put this towards the bills." I explained as I handed her two small bundles of cash.

"Okay, no problem." she responded before getting off the sofa to put the money away.

****

The following day I picked up Mugs at his house out in Rosedale, Queens at about 11 AM.

"What's up brethren?" he greeted me as he got into the van.

"Everything cool? Y ou alright?"

"Yeah man, everything good, so what's on the agenda for today?"

"Well I got a couple people working inside a few Radio Shacks and No Body Beats The Wiz Electronic stores, so we are just going to go to a couple of them and buy some computers, phones and other electronics with some credit cards."

"What about the ID? You ain't make none for me?"

"We ain't going to need any. I just want you to hang out with me, watch and get to meet my peoples, so I don't have to keep going into these store all the time, besides all I got to do is buy them something off the card for helping me."

"Alright then, this shit sounds easy lets roll." he said as I pulled out, heading back to the Belt PKWY heading back towards Brooklyn.

Over the next couple months I had Mugs working with me mostly everyday. He was a quick learner, but I could tell he was not happy with this type of hustle. Mugs had been a robber and drug dealer all of his life and he was used to getting that fast money in lump sums. I wasn't surprised when we were riding around shopping one day and he said to me " Yo Dread, I got a jux I want you to do with me."

"Yeah, where at?"

"Up in Connecticut."

"Tell me about it."

"There is this Jamaican dude named Ronnie up there that's

Enemies Amongst Us   D. Isaac

moving allot of weed. He brings about 400 pounds or more at a time from Texas. He be bringing the weed up stashed in the middle of stacks of lumber shipments on tractor trailers every month."

"How you know all this?"

"I'm cool with one of his boys that works for him and he told me about their whole operation. You see dude don't be treating his crew right he is a cheap mutha fucka and my boy said he'd help us rob him for a cut."

"A'ight, shit sounds good so far."

"I want us to drive up to Connecticut so we can scope out dude's house and see how he operates."

"A'ight, we can do that tomorrow." I told him, as he got happy about the prospect of getting back on familiar ground and getting some big money.

"But we are going to do this my way." I finished.

"That's cool with me." he replied.

    The next day my boy Black from the island of Guyana drove up to Connecticut with us. The Jamaican dude, Ronnie, lived on a quiet street behind some sort of factory. He lived in small one family house with his wife and four kids. Directly across the street from him house sitting on some grass was a load of plywood, about 10 stacks with about 50 sheets a piece.

"Yo Starr, this boy must be crazy! He bring this shit right here in front of his house out in the open." I said, not believing my eyes. Then again it did make a little sense if you put something out in

Enemies Amongst Us   D. Isaac

plain sight nobody would pay any attention to it right? If you tried to hide it then everybody wants to know what your hiding. You couldn't pull a stunt like this in NYC though, because the crack heads would've taken all of the plywood while you slept.

After watching Ronnie operate for about 2 weeks, I decided that I'd seen enough to make my move. He didn't bring his customers to his house. He sold his weed out of a bar and a game room that he hung out at a few minutes away from where he lived at.

To be a good stick up artist you must have patience and you must put in your time doing surveillance work, just like the police would do. I had bought walkie talkies, police scanners, a book that had all the police frequencies in the United States, and binoculars. These are some of the essential tools a professional robber needs.

It was on a Rainey Saturday night, I decided to rob Ronnie up in Connecticut. In just a short time of watching dude, I'd learned he liked to hang out late on Friday and Saturday nights. I wanted to catch him coming home after he had been out drinking. Another of my reason was when the weather was bad people tend to let their guards down. They were busy worrying about getting wet and out of the rain leaving themselves vulnerable to wolves like myself. I called Mugsy and told him and Black to meet up with me so we could pursue the job. Then I decided to call Carlos and Rocky as well, to run extra security.

"What's up rude boy?" I asked, when Mugsy answered his phone.

"Just chillin." He replied.

"Where you at?"

Enemies Amongst Us
D. Isaac

"I'm chilling with one of my ladies at her crib out in Canarsie."

"Yo, I'm ready to drive up to Connecticut and go handle that situation."

"Starr me ah chill with me girl and me naah come out." He replied in his thick Jamaican accent.

"A'ight, I'ma chat to you later." I told, him ending the call.

"What did he say?" Black asked, after I'd hung up the phone.

"He said he was chilling with one of his girls and he wasn't coming."

"So what's that mean for us?"

"It means I'm gonna get two of my other boy and we're gonna go up there and handle out business. Fuck Mugs. One monkey don't stop my show."

"I know that's right." I called up boy Carlos and he told me to swing by his crib and pick him up when I was ready. Next I called my boy Rocky, who I had met upstate at Clinton Max Prison back in the days. Rocky was from Jamaica and was always bragging about being a gun man and how he used to roll with the Untouchables back in the days in Flatbush, so I decided to take him along because I knew he needed the money. He had just come home from prison after doing 15 years up north and he was broke.

Carlos rode with me in my car and Rocky was riding with Black in his Honda Civic. By the time we made it out to Connecticut it was about 10 PM and it was dark and still raining. The Jamaican dude's car was not parked in front of his house or anywhere on his block. He was out hanging out like I had anticipated. Black parked his car on the corner of the street, while I parked in front of a house a couple doors down the street, and waited for him to come home.

I had never done a robbery with Rocky before and I wanted to see how he would behave under pressure. Some dudes be talking that gangster stuff, but when it comes time to walk the walk they fold up when the heat is on. My two main boys LA and Shameek was still away in prison and I had eased up on the home invasion since they've been gone. Now that Mugs had put the thought back into my head, I knew I would have to break in a new crew.

While waiting on Ronnie to come back I laid out the plan to my boys.

"Yo Black, you and Carlos rush dude when he starts going into his house. Rocky you back them up and help them tie up everybody that's inside. Make sure ya'll clear the house before you start searching for the loot." I told them.

"We got you Big Dogg." They replied in unison.

I had given Black one of the walkie talkies before we had left Brooklyn so we could communicate. It was about 2 AM when the Jamaican finally came home, and he had his girlfriend with him. He had taken her out to party with him. They both looked a little drunk, stumbling out of the car and towards the house together with that tipsy swag that develops after a couple drinks.

I didn't have time to teach Black about talking in codes on the walkie talkies so I just told him.

"Yo Son, tell Rocky to get the girl and move now."

Enemies Amongst Us   D. Isaac

Carlos was already on the move outside my car, Black and Rocky came up behind the couple and forced them inside the house. It went like clock-work in less than a minute they had the couple inside their house without making a scene or firing a shot. Most drug dealer, especially Jamaicans, carried guns on them. They are known to be trigger happy so one has to be very careful running up on them trying to rob them.

As I'm sitting in my car watching out for the police and listening to the police scanner in case some nosey neighbor might've see something and called the police, I see Rocky running back out of the door and straight for my car.

"What's up Rude Boy, what happened?" I asked, him thinking something must've gone wrong inside the house.

"Starr, they got four kids in there and two of them was sleeping. I can't tie up no kids." He said trembling.

I could tell Rocky was really afraid, so I told him.

"Yo just sit in the car and look out and listen for the police, call me on the radio if you hear them coming." I explained.   Then spoke into the radio.

"Yo son, I'm coming in." So Black would have the heads up I was on my way.

"Yo stay out there we on the way out." came the reply as him and Carlos walked out the door each carrying shopping bags.

When we got back to the stash house in Brooklyn, I said to Black and Carlos.

Enemies Amongst Us

D. Isaac

"Yo, what the fuck happened?"

The both looked at Rocky then back at me before Carlos replied.

"Your man bitched the fuck out, panicked and ran out the house leaving us to do all the work. That's what happened."

"Yeah he ain't getting shit." Black added as he started counting the money and splitting it into three piles.

"What you mean I ain't getting shit?" Rocky asked, eyeing the three growing piles of cash envious that there wasn't a fourth.

"Exactly what I said. You ran out on us in the middle of a jux, left the door wide open and you think you deserve a cut? You must've bumped your mutha fuckin head. Where do they do that at?" Black spat, spewing venom and staring at him straight in the eyes before glancing at me to see if I was in agreement.

"Yo, Rocky the mans right. You fucked up. You got to carry your own weight on this team. You can't expect mutha fuckas to do all the work then break you off after they risk their lives. Nah rude boy it can't go so. Besides because of your scary ass we had to abandon the jux mid-way through and didn't even get to search the spot properly and definitely left behind some of what we went there for in the first place."

Black and Carlos had come out with $60,000 in cash and 30 pounds of some Bomb Skunk Weed. After we split everything three ways it was $20,000 and 10 pound each.

"Yo, I need a G ($1,000) from each of ya'll to give to Mugs for putting us on this lick, he is going to cry if we don't break him off proper, plus right is right."

"A'ight" they both agreed as they each counted, then handed me a stack of crisp bills.

Once everybody was ready to leave I asked Rocky to hang behind. Carlos and Black took off and I told Rocky.

"Sit down." and started counting out some bills then handed them to him.

"Here's a grand and I'll give you a pound of weed out of my cut. You don't deserve it but your my man and I fuck with you."

"Thanks Dread." He said, humbly looking up at me.

"A'ight now get your shit and get the fuck out of my house I need some rest I'm heading to Atlantic City tomorrow."

Chapter 19

After the jux with Black, Carlos and Rocky I kicked back with Brittney as we welcomed our precious gift into the world. More responsibilities were born and I became like a wind storm. Anything in my way was getting blew through. I loved my life and wouldn't trade it for the world. When I would think things are tightening up, money comes raining in my lap. Home was good and my new baby boy needed everything I could think of so I got back to the money.

I had been going down to Atlantic city in New Jersey for a

Enemies Amongst Us   D. Isaac

couple years on short get always with Brenda. I had become a VIP member at the Bally's Park Place Casino. Whenever I was going down to A.C. I would call up my good friend Pierre, the casino host.

"Yo Pierre, this Dex what's up playboy?" I greeted him when he answered the phone.

"Good afternoon Mr.Isaac, how are you today?" He responded, professionally like his boss was eaves dropping, then added "Will you be coming down this evening Sir?"

"Yeah I'm coming down as a matter of fact I'm on the road right now."

"How many people in your party sir?"

"I got three of my boys with me and I will be needing two rooms."

"How long will you be staying with us?"

"About two or three days."

"Alright sir, everything is all set. I will see you when you get here."

"Thanks Pierre." I said, ending the call.

Pierre was my casino host at Bally's. We had become friends over the past couple years. He had hooked me up with a few of his friends that worked in the credit cards cash advance cages in a couple casinos through-out the city.

In 1997 I found myself going down to Atlantic for the black

Enemies Amongst Us   D. Isaac

jack tables like a junky picks up an addiction for drugs. I just couldn't get enough of the place known as "America's Favorite Playground."

Sometimes when I came down to Atlantic City, I would bring a couple of my friends to do cash advances for me. I would bring 20-30 credit cards and activate them in my hotel room, then send my crew to the booths that Pierre had his friends working at that day.

Doing cash advances with credit cards was the sweetest money I ever made. All I had to do was go to a machine in the casino, swipe the card and punch in how much money I wanted to withdraw. Once the amount was approved, I would then send one of my friends to the cash advance cages to sign for and pick up the money. They would show the person in the cage a fake ID for the cameras sake, then collect the money and leave.

We would do this all day until I got almost all of the money off from every card I had with me. Later on when I met with Pierre, I would give him $300 from each card we used. He'd take thirty percent on the top and distribute the rest to the people that worked in the cages. Everybody wins, everybody's happy.

After me and my boys had checked into our rooms, we went on down to the casino floor to hit the tables. On my way there I ran into Pierre.

"Yo Pierre what's up fly guy? I see you looking real sharp, as usual." Pierre was about 5'8" light skinned, slim built and curly hair. He was always immaculately dressed in tailored suits. while he worked the casino. He could pass for a GQ model.

"What's happening Dee? You know I got to represent ." He replied. Pierre was the youngest casino host in Atlantic City.

"These are my boys Carlos, Black and Mugsy y'all meet man man Pierre." I said, introducing them all.

After the introductions were made Pierre said " Yo Dee, let me have a word with you in private for a minute please. Pulling me off to the side.

"What's up Baby Boy." I asked once we were alone.

"Did you bring any cards with you?" he asked cutting straight to business.

"Nah man, I just came down here to chill and relax for a couple days this time."

"Damn, I wanted new rims for my ride." He said, the disappointment clear in his voice.

"I got you next week when I come back down, don't trip my man."

"For real?"

"Yeah I got you."

"A'ight then, go hit the tables and win some money this time. Let me know when you get hungry so I can get you some comp tickets for you and the crew to eat."

"Okay I will check you out later then." I told him and headed to the tables to win some money.

Enemies Amongst Us   D. Isaac

After a couple hours of gambling, I decided to take a break. As me and my boys were walking into the restaurant I ran into an old associate from my past.

"Yo Dread, what's happening with you my man? How you doing?"

It was Mike, this west Indian dude from Brooklyn that I had met through Sly and Buddy.

"What's up Mike? Long time no see." I said, greeting him.

"Man Dread, it's good to see you, man you look like your doing good for yourself. What you been up to?"

"Well right now Mike we getting ready to get something to eat."

"Can I tag along man, I'm broke and starving like Marvin." He said, as he stared at the floor shamefully.

"Sure Mike, why not come on." I said, then added "Meet my boys Carlos , Black and Mugsy." once again making introductions.

After we had all eaten, we went back to my room to relax for a little while. Carlos had taking a liking to mike so Mike had once again tagged along with us.

While we were chilling in the room Mike said "Yo Dread, I got this dude that wants to buy two kilos of cocaine."

The room gets deadly quiet after he made the statement. I had not mentioned to Mike that I was into selling drugs. He just jumped out there assuming that was what me and my boys were up to. When I looked around the room ,all of my boys had their eyes on me. It was like all of our robbers sensors had just been activated at the same time. I didn't have to say anything. I already knew what the three of them was thinking by the look in their eyes.

"Yo, Mike where is this dude at?" I asked him.

"He lives out here." He said, then finished "I told him I can get them two keys for $25,000 each."

"I'ma have to go back to Brooklyn, get it and then bring it back down."

"That's cool, I didn't expect you to have it on you. Just call me when you get back." He said giving me his cell number then added "Then I'll make all the arrangements to get this deal done."

I had to cut my trip short and we drove back to Brooklyn that night. When we all got inside my stash house the first thing out of Mugsy's mouth was.

"How we gonna do this Dex?"

I had been thinking about this for the last hour and forty five minutes it took me to drive back.

"This is the plan, I'm gonna make two of my dummy kilo's up, when we go back down we'll rent a room in one of the cheap motels on the strip and tell Mike to bring the dude there, or we go to his crib and bag him there."

"Who is going to drive the guns down the highway?" Black asked, worrying because he was still on parole and didn't want to be caught with a gun on the road. The New Jersey troopers are notorious for profiling their highway.

Enemies Amongst Us   D. Isaac

"I will get my Jamaican girl Michelle to drive them down along with the fake bricks in her car." I said.

Michelle was a Red-Bone cutie that was always down for some action, as long as there was a pay day at the end of it. She was always asking me to take her on robberies with me or if I knew anybody she could have sex with to set them up and rob them. The girl was a stone cold pretty gangster. Many hustlers had fallen victim to her pretty face and charms, thinking with their dick rather than brains. This mistake costs many men dearly.

Early the next morning all three of my boys called me asking what time we were leaving. I had been trying all night to come up with a plan to leave two of them behind. It was only a $50,000 dollars job and I didn't want to split that four ways after breaking Michelle off for driving the guns back and foth. No matter what I thought, I just couldn't come up with a good enough excuse to shake them. Plus they were all on me to go, eventually I said fucked it and we all hit the highway around 11AM heading back down the Garden State PKWY back to Atlantic City.

When we got back down there, I had Michelle rent a room in a motel a couple blocks from Bally's. Then I called Mike.

"Yo Mike, what's up? I'm back and I got that for you player." I said when he answered his phone.

"A'ight Dread, let me call my man and set things up, I'll get back to you ASAP."

About an hour later Mike calls back "Yo Dread, my man said to get a sample from you so he could check it out."

"Alright meet me on the boardwalk outside the Taj Mahal

Enemies Amongst Us   D. Isaac

casino in 20 minutes." I told him.

When he arrived, I gave him a gram of some real good fish-scale cocaine and he told me he would call me back in a little while. About an hour went by before his next call.

"Yo Dread, he wants me to see the two bricks with my eyes before he'll do it."

"What?" I snapped, clearly frustrated. then added "What type of fucking games your boy playing Mike?"

"This is my first time doing business with him Dread, and he is just being paranoid that's all"

"I thought you knew this dude? How you know he ain't the police?" I asked.

"Dread he ain't the police, I swear."

"You sure?"

"Yeah I'm sure. I'd bet my life on it." He responded.

"A'ight then meet me in front of the Tropicana in 15 minutes."

When Mike showed up, I take him up to the room we had rented in the motel. He looked nervous when he saw Michelle and my three boys sitting around the room with their guns out.

"Go on in there." I said, as I pushed him in his back, coming in behind him and locking the door.

"No need to be nervous Mike, I'm just a little paranoid too." I explained, as I opened up Michelle's bag and showed him the two

Enemies Amongst Us   D. Isaac

dummy kilos inside.

"I sure hope you ain't make me go through all this trouble bringing this stuff all the way down here to be playing games Mike."

"Nah Dread, you know me and I wouldn't do that to you man. I'm going and gonna

tell him that everything is legit so we could make this happen and get the deal over with. I'ma call you right back when I get to his house." Mike said, as he exited the room.

We waited for Mike to call back and when I didn't hear from him after a few hours I knew something wasn't right and we went back to Bally's

About 10 PM that night, I ran into Pierre on the casino floor. He was getting ready to get off work, so we went up to my room to kick it.

"What's up Dee? You look kinda stressed out about something. You lost a lot of money again?" He asked, once we were all sitting around in my room.

"Nah Pierre, but I sure feel like I did."

"What's wrong with you then?"

"I was getting ready to rob this Sucker with two dummy kilos of cocaine, but he didn't come through with the money. The mutha fucka left me hanging."

"Get the fuck out of here." Pierre said, getting all excited. In all reality Pierre was really a good kid, but he was fascinated with the gangster lifestyle that I was living, so I wasn't surprised by what he said next.

"Yo Dee, can I see the dummy kilos?"

I just looked at him and busted out laughing.

"Sure why not. Michelle give my boy them bricks from out of your bag." I told her watching Pierre.

Pierre's eyes were glued to Michelle's phat ass when she went to get the dummy bricks out of her bag across the room. I felt sorry for him, if only he knew. Michelle would've eaten his little square ass alive. Some women were just as ruthless as men. When she handed the bricks, she smiled showing off her dimples and gold teeth. He lit up like a Christmas tree.

"Yo Dee, what are you going to do with these now that your deal didn't work out?"

"Get rid of them before I hit the highway." I said.

"Can I have them?" He asked, looking at the two fake bricks like they were a special souvenir or something.

"What are you going to do with them Pierre?"

"I don't know yet, but I want them.

"A'ight you can have them, just don't do anything stupid and get your ass in any trouble."

"I won't." He promised.

"A'ight we out. I'll see you this weekend. Make sure you get me two of them tickets for the Felix Trinidad fight. I'm bringing my new wife back down with me, we starting to beef cause I haven't been taking her out.

"Don't even trip, I got you and I'm gonna reserve a room for you before we get booked out." He said giving me a brotherly hug before we parted.

Enemies Amongst Us   D. Isaac

Chapter 20

    I had been ripping and running in the streets and had been neglecting my responsibilities to Brittney. I had made her my new wifey after the break up with Brenda, and moved her and my new baby into a two bedroom apartment in a two family house in Canarsie. After the incident at the condo with Brenda, I couldn't risk her just popping up on me like that again. I had bought Brittney a grey four door Nissan Stanza so she could drive back and forth to work and also a black Mercedes C280 for her to style in on the weekends.

    We had a healthy relationship going, once she began working again. I wanted her to save her money, so I paid all the bills in our home. I had always felt that this was the mans job in a relationship. The man should be the bread winner and provide for his family. That's how all the men with families that I knew growing up in Trinidad were carrying it. This is what I saw as a youngster growing up there, and also when I first came to America back in the days when my mother and I lived with her husband Karl. That was one of the things he taught me and it stayed with me.

    Brittney was very happy when I told her that I was taking her to Atlantic City for the weekend. I promised her that I was going to take her to watch the fight, then go to the after party, and also hit up some local clubs to do some dancing with her. My baby was so happy that she left work early Friday to go get some new outfits, and get her hair and nails done proper.

    When we stepped out of Bally's that Saturday night to go to see the fight my baby had guys and girls both checking her out. She was looking so sexy in her mini leather skirt with matching knee high leather boots. I was not doing to bad myself in a double breasted midnight blue two piece suit with my blue Mauri alligator shoes and matching alligator belt. Also I had on my gangster Derby hat, Cartier shades and the black and blue faced ice-out Rolex from the Tito lick.

After watching Felix Trinidad beat up on his opponent. I didn't feel like partying anymore because my gambling disease had kicked in and I could hear the tables screaming my name. I whispered in Brittney's ear.

"Baby let's go play some black jack for a little while until the clubs gets jumping."

"Okay." she agreed "But just for a little while, because you know how you get." she finished skeptically.

That little while turned into the fastest 5 hours man has ever seen. After the first 2 hours Brittney got mad because of the money I'd lost and not wanting to leave the table and go to the clubs.

"Dee, come on you promised." she nagged, as she tugged my sleeve.

"Why don't you give me a break for a little while. I think your jinxing me or something." I snapped back at her.

After I'd made that statement, Brittney stormed out of the casino and went upstairs to our room.

It was about 3 AM before I'd lost all of my money, pawned my Rolex, lost that money to, and crept back into our room.

Enemies Amongst Us   D. Isaac

"Baby you up?" I called to her knowing she had heard me when I came in the room, and that she was playing sleep because she was mad at me.

"No Dee, I'm sleeping." she responded, rolling over turning her back towards me.

"Baby I'm sorry." I said then added " You know I love you with all my heart." as she just laid there not saying a word, trying to ignore me.

"Baby, I need some money from you." I said.

"What?" she snapped in disbelief. Finally, I had her attention.

"I lost all my money baby and I need you to give me a thousand until we get home." I pleaded, not realizing how bad the gambling had gotten a hold of me like a drug.

"How bad do you want it?" she asked, rolling over peeping at me.

"I want it real bad Baby." I said, not knowing where she was going asking me this.

"Then you got to eat my pussy if you want it." she said, watching me closely to see how I was going to respond to this.

"Girl stop playing with me. You know I'm a Rasta. I don't eat no damn blood-clat pussy."

"You ain't no real Rasta Dee. You just got dreads that's all."

She knew I didn't get down like that, eating no damn pussy, but she was mad at me for not taking her out to party and she was ready to take full advantage of my gambling jones.

"I ain't playing." she continued "If you want me to give you this money then you got to eat it."

"A'ight you wanna play me like that, come on and take off all your clothes." I told her plotting on her ass.

She flew out of bed and was back laying butt naked spread eagle on the bed in the blink of an eye, smiling at me like she'd just hit the jackpot downstairs. I kept all my clothes on except for my shoes and suit jacket and got in the bed next to her.

"You know West Indian men don't do this right." I told her, while kissing her lightly on her lips and sucking on her tongue.

"Boy please, that's what ya'll say to each other when ya'll be hanging out with ya'll friends, but I know better." she said, starting to breath hard.

"Oh yeah?"

"Yeah, now get down there and handle your business if you want this money." she said, grabbing my dreads and pushing my head down.

I started licking on her breasts slowly one at a time while blowing on the tip of her nipple forcing her to moan out.

"Yes baby, yesssss." she moaned, as her fingers threaded through my hair and she held me close to her chest while I sucked long and hard on her perfect size tits. She tasted so sweet I had to control myself not to explode in my pants.

As I kissed a path down the warm skin of her belly to the sweet heat of her thighs, I ran my fingers over her moist opening and she gasped.

"Ohhh Dee, ooh baby."

As I tasted her sweet nectar her muscles relaxed and her legs spread wider. I cupped her ass and tilted her for better access. At the first flick of my tongue she moved her hips and tightened her grip on my dreads begging me for more.

"Yes baby, that's it, that's it baby right there baby." she begged.

I licked her softly, then slowly at first until I had her soaking wet and in that zone of ultimate ecstasy. Then I started going fast and using my teeth on her. Suddenly she pushed my head away and cried out.

"Stop, stop Dee, you don't know what your doing. You getting ready to scar up my pussy. Just take the money and go." she screamed as she got up and handed me the bills

"Thanks Baby." I said, as I went into the bathroom to brush my teeth and laugh at her. That was the easiest thousand bucks I ever made. I was back downstairs in 10 minutes winning back all the money I had lost earlier.

Brittney thought she was doing something slick by trying to get me to eat her pussy, but I bet she wouldn't ask me to do that shit again after I put them teeth on her smart ass.

Chapter 21

When I arrived back in Brooklyn from hanging out with Brittney in Atlantic City, I decided to get back on track with my credit cards hustling. Things just weren't going good for me doing stick ups, since the loss of Shameek and LA. My new crew just wasn't clicking right for some reason.

My boy Black was into burglarizing houses, and one day he came by my stash house after he had finished a lick in Flatbush. He had found a few credit cards and didn't know what to do with them. I took him with me to a couple of Radio Shack stores that I had people working at. We bought a couple computers, stereos, fax machines, and a wide assortment of other electronic gadgets. After we had pushed all the cards to their limit, I drove into Times Square in Manhattan, where I knew this Syrian Electronic store owner who would buy electronics for half of the retail cost then re-sell them in his store for the full price. I sold him everything Black and I had and we split the money down the middle. After that Black was hooked, wide open to the card hustle and I couldn't get rid of him.

He started hanging out with me so much that whenever I would get credit cards from my connects, I would sell him a few of them so he could get his hustle on also.

Mean while Marilyn had opened up a new real estate office on 5th AVE, in the Park Slope section of Brooklyn. I took Black with me there one afternoon, so I could use her computer to run some credit reports on the names that were on the new cards I had just purchased.

Enemies Amongst Us — D. Isaac

"Sak pase Cherrie? Comment allez-vous?" I greeted her, in her native language Creole, while kissing her on both cheeks.

"M'ap boule." she responded, giving me one of her trademark smiles.

"Dee, I want you to meet somebody." she said getting up from her desk taking me into the back office.

"Dee this is my husband Sayeed, Sayeed this is the very good friend of mines Dee that I've told you about." Marilyn introduced us.

I was in complete shock. I knew Marilyn had a boyfriend, but she didn't tell me she went and got married, and to an Arab at that.

"Salam Walaikum." I greeted him in Arabic.

"Walaikum Salam." Sayeed responded, looking surprised at me for greeting him in Arabic.

"It's a pleasure to finally meet you Dee." He said, while shaking my hand.

"Same to you." I responded.

"Dee I was just getting ready to make salaat, so could you please excuse me for a few minutes."

"Sure Sayeed, I got some business to handle with Marilyn anyway. Take your time."

When Marilyn and I returned to the front of the store, I started interrogating her.

Enemies Amongst Us   D. Isaac

"Marilyn how long you known this dude?"

"I met him a couple of years ago Dee."

"You in love with him?"

"I married him didn't I?"

"He looks kinda sneaky, like one of them Taliban mutha fuckas."

"Every Muslim is not a terrorist Dee."

"A'ight then once your happy, I'm happy. By the way I want you to meet my friend Black, Black meet Marilyn." I said, introducing them before continuing.

"Baby girl I need to use the computer to run some reports."

"Go handle your business Dee, but make sure you give me my money before you leave this time."

"Okay baby I got you.

Before I had started doing business with my boy Squeeze, Marilyn had introduced me to two African dudes from Nigeria. Their names were SP and Patrick and these dudes were the real deal when it came to checks and credit cards. I'm talking real professionals. They taught me all the in's and out's about this hustle. Once they told me that in there home town in Nigeria. There was actually was a school that taught how to commit fraud in America and abroad. My African boys had showed me how to get fake drivers licenses that were so good that the only way somebody would know it was fake were to run a check through the DMV database. They taught me all the ways to activate new credit cards and how to obtain someone's mothers maiden name and social security numbers. Two of the key security elements you must have to activate most credit cards.

Once I received all the information that I needed to activate all forty credit cards, I gave Marilyn her $2,000 and we left.

"Yo son, we going to use these cards today?" Black asked, once we were loaded back in my car. READ HERE

"Nah this is what we are going to do. I'm gonna rent a sixteen passenger van in the morning and we will take out a couple of seat in the back so we have room to stack all our stuff, then I will grab a couple of my people and we will drive down to that big shopping mall in Virginia and work our way back up hitting every mall and shopping outlet in DC, Maryland, Atlantic City, and through out New Jersey until all the cards are burnt up." I explained.

"Yeah, I'm with that." Black responded, beaming at me with anticipation.

"Yo, listen we are gonna split the bill on the car rental fee and you got to break my people off for working your cards for you."

"That's cool Dee. I got that."

The next day four of us hit the New Jersey Turnpike heading south. I had brought my home girl form Jamaica, Sonia, and my homie Mike along on the trip to shop for us. Sonia was a beast when it came to shopping. She would dress up in a white nurses uniform along with white shoes and even a stethoscope hanging around her neck while she would shop. the cashiers in the stores never asked her for ID when she went up to purchase her items with credit cards or checks. They would just assume she was a

Enemies Amongst Us
D. Isaac

nurse or doctor and give her the purchases without any problems.

Mike was 6' 2" dark skinned, an immaculate dressing, articulate homo-sexual. He loved to shop, and when he was out shopping he never had any problems due to his way with words and friendly demeanor when dealing with people. Mike was very keen in seeking out other homo-sexuals working when he was shopping then getting them to assist him while he shopped with the fraudulent cards.

After two days of shopping at all of the malls and outlets along interstate 95 that passed through Virginia, Georgetown in Washington DC, and Maryland, I decided to stop by Atlantic City for a couple of hours on the way back home to burn up the rest of the credit cards we hadn't finished using.

After securing the van in the parking garage at Bally's Park Place Casino, we went to find my boy Pierre.

"What's up playboy?" I greeted him, when I found him at work on the casino floor.

"A'int nothing Dee, just another day grinding in the cotton field, you know me. What you and your peeps up to? Ya'll checked in already?"

"Nah man, we ain't staying, just passing through real quick. I got a couple of cards that I'm trying to burn up and get back on the highway."

"Oh yeah? I got my boy Pete working the cash advance cage down at the Taj Majal and my boy Roy working the cage at The Harrah's right now."

Enemies Amongst UsD. Isaac

"That sounds just great, why don't you give them a call and let them know we're on our way to see them."

"Okay, let me handle that, aye Dee you ain't forgot me on them rims I told you I needed right?"

"Nah pierre, of course not. I'ma break you off proper before we dip."

After we got $15,000 in cash advances, and I had lost $5,000 of it playing black jack, I was ready to leave before I lost everything I'd brought. When I met back up with Pierre at Bally's I gave him $2,100 to split with his people.

"Aye Dee, you got anymore cards left with money on them?"

"Yeah I got a couple Pierre, what's on your mind?"

"Dee, I told you I'm trying to get some rims for my car."

"Pierre I don't want you going into any stores with these credit cards! You might get caught and lose your job."

"Dee you ain't gotta worry about that. I'ma get one of my people to do it for me." He said sincerely.

I didn't want to give Pierre the cards, but after looking at him and his pleading eyes, I went against my better judgment and gave him two cards that had about $2,500 each left on them.

" Yo man don't do anything foolish with these cards and get your ass in trouble. I'll see you next week." I said to him as we left the casino towards the van, ready to head back up to the Garden State Parkway all the way to the NYC.

Enemies Amongst Us   D. Isaac

Chapter 22

I enjoyed myself in Atlantic City even though I lost a couple of dollars. "When it comes fast it goes fast" is what I've always been told. Now back at home i felt like I was on vacation. The wifey was always happy when I walk through the door after being away for a few days or even sometimes a week.

Only two days back from Atlantic City and I'm wanting to go back. I lost the $5,000 and I need to get my money back, I wasn't the loser type and losing isn't part of my M.O. I always win whether it takes a day or a decade, I always come out on top. I didn't want to drive back alone, so I hit up one of my big homies Big Dread.

I met Big Dread while I was locked up at Arthur Kill Correctional Facility on Staten Island a couple years back. We had become friends not just because he was from Trinidad also, but because big Dread was a real likeable dude. At first glance one might be intimidated by his appearance, because he was really a big dude. big Dread was about 6'6" dark complexion with long dread locks that reached the middle of his back. He was about 300 pounds but was what some would refer to as a gentle giant once you got to know him. Big Dread had just come home from prison and I was hanging out with him and Rocky when I got a call form Carlos on my cell.

"What up Dex, what you up to?" He asked when i answered.

"Ain't nothing rude boy, just chillin with my boys big Dread and

Rocky." I replied.

"Yo Son, I'm in town for a couple days and shit, lets do something." He said.

"you feel like riding down to Atlantic City to chill for a day or so? I need to see Pierre anyway" I asked.

"Yeah that sounds good. What time you want to pull out?"

"Give me about two hours and im going to come by your crib, we'll leave from there. Yo I'm bringing Rocky and my boy with us," I explained. Carlos had met Rocky before, but had not met Big Dread since he'd been out.

"A'ight, im going to see you when you get here." He said ending the call.

After I had swung by Rocky and big Dreads cribs so they could grab a change of clothing. I get a call from Mugsy.

"Yo Dex, where you at?" He asked, sounding upset like something was bothering him.

"I'm on my way to my crib for some clothes. Me and a couple of the fellas are going down to Atlantic City to chill for a couple days." I told him.

"Yo, I'm going to meet you at your crib in a few minutes." I need to switch cars with you." He said.

"A'ight." I replied. I didn't mind driving Mugsy's car when I was going out of town. I just didn't like driving it around the City because it drew to much attention.

Enemies Amongst Us   D. Isaac

When I met up with Mugsy at my house, I could see that he was really upset by his demeanor so I pulled him aside.

"Yo Son, what's wrong with you? What you tripping on?"

"Yo man, Cheryl is cheating on me with some nigga that drives a big green Benz like mines."

"Get the fuck out of here." I responded then added "How do you know?"

"Paulie saw them and called me. She ah fuck some blud-clat Yankee boy that lives over by Rochdale Village where Paulie be getting his hair cut on Guy-Brewer Blvd." He said in his thick Jamaican accent.

"Damn rude-boy, that's fucked up." I said, ever since Mugs had gotten on his feet and bought his big body Benz he had been fucking a whole lot of females and had not been spending any time with his wife. Like most men, myself included, he felt it was alright to cheat on his woman, but it was a crime for her to do the same. Wifeys are not supposed to cheat. Plain and simple.

"Yo, I'm going to follow her around in your car and catch her in the act."

"A'ight man, just don't go killing anybody in my damn car Mugs."

"Nah Dex, I ain't gonna do all that. I'm just gonna spy on her slick ass a little bit."

After I had finished with Mugsy, we went by Carlos's crib in Crown Heights and Rocky jumped into his car with him and we hit

Enemies Amongst Us   D. Isaac

the Garden State Parkway to drive down to Atlantic City.

I had called Pierre form the car when we were on the highway and had him reserve two rooms in my name for us at Bally's.

When we arrived at the casino I went over to the concierge desk and got our room keys. I gave Big Dread and Rocky a set of keys for their room and Carlos and I kept a set for ours.

I had given Big Dread a thousand dollars as a coming home present and he brought half of it with him, so he could have some pocket money to play with in case he got lucky. Carlos had given Rocky some pocket money also, cause he knew he wasn't doing to good and Rocky wouldn't of asked him for any because he was full of pride. This was one the reasons I liked Carlos. He was a genuine dude. He was not selfish with his money. He would help a complete stranger on streets if he felt they needed help, even if they didn't ask.

Later on that night while we were sitting at the bar taking a break from the black jack tables and slot machines, Carlos noticed two beautiful young ladies checking us out.

"Yo, son, I'm going to kick it with them two shorties over there and see what's up with them." He said, getting up and going over to where the two girls were standing.

While Carlos was talking to the girls, I said to Big Dread and Rocky "Twenty dollars says each of those girls are broke over there."

"Why you say that Dex?" Big Dread asked.

"Man, I damn near live in these casinos, I'm down here every week. I can tell by looking in peoples eyes when they are winning or losing. When you see people just standing around looking lost and not drinking any of this free liquor, most likely their ass done got broke and they trying to figure out how to get their hands on some more loot." I explained.

A few minutes later Carlos came back over and sat down.

"What's up with them shorties rude-boy?" Big Dread asked.

"Their names are Lisa and Shirley and they are from Pennsylvania. They done lost all their money and are trying to figure out what to do." Carlos replied.

"What did I say. I told Ya'll I can spot them a mile away." I said.

"Yo, ya'll trying to get some pussy from them or what? Carlos asked.

Carlos was a real ladies man, he was forever plotting on how to get into every woman's drawers. My boy did not discriminate. If she was short, tall, skinny, fat, ugly or fine, my boy was trying to fuck. He just didn't care. One thing about him though was, I never saw him step to a white chick. So I guess that's where he drew his line. My dude was only sticking to the sisters.

"Hell yeah." Bid Dread and Rocky both said at the same time.

My mind was getting back to the Black Jack tables. When I came down here I came to gamble and try to win some money not to chase pussy. The only time that I wanted to fuck and party was after I'd made some loot and that had not happened yet on this trip. To be honest I was actually down a couple racks.

Enemies Amongst Us   D. Isaac

"Yo ya'll go ahead I'ma head back to the tables." I said.

"Nah Dex, we came down here to have some fun together. You could always gamble when you come down here solo." Carlos pleaded, looking at me to see how I'd react.

"A'ght your right." I said giving in, not wanting to be a party pooper.

"Listen, let me go hook this up with them, so we can all get some." Carlos said, heading back over to the ladies table.

About 10 minutes later Carlos came back and said.

"Okay here is the plan, how much money ya'll got left?"

"Starr, all I got left is about fifty dollars buck rude-boy." Rocky said, in his deep Jamaican accent.

Big Dread added "I got a hundred left."

They all looked at me at the same time cause I had not said anything.

"Ya'll tripping, I ain't got no money to be buying pussy. My money is to gamble with." I said shaking my head with disappointment at them.

"Come on Dex, stop being so fucking tight and loosen up, have some fucking fun with us. I got it, damn! here is the plan. You see the tall one, that looks like Serena Williams, she wants $200 and she's with it. Rocky and Big Dread ya'll got her, just take her to your room and handle y'all business. Dex, me and you got the other one with the long wavy hair, I told her we'd buy her some shoes from the boutique in the lobby.

Enemies Amongst Us   D. Isaac

"Damn Carlos, she is fine as shit, but do you know how much clothes cost in that boutique?" I asked, him knowing he didn't have a clue how expensive that boutique was. All the stores inside the casinos always had name brand designer wear, and the mark up they put on it was unreal. Most of their customers were high rollers that came through and the didn't care about prices.

"Don't trip son, I got this. Lets go up to the room and have some fun." He said.

We had two rooms on the 18th floor of the casino with a very nice view of the Atlantic Ocean. Our room came with double beds and when we got there Carlos decided her wanted to take a shower, so I went and laid on one of the bed. The girl that Carlos had chosen for us was named Lisa and she looked at me, smiled, and said.

"Do you want me to come over there and give you a massage? You look kinda tense baby you alright?"

I studied her features for a couple minutes and I realized she was one of those naturally beautiful women. She didn't need or have on any make up. Her complexion was like a red cherry, she could pass for a Native Americans, and with all that long wavy hair I wouldn't be surprised if she had some Cherokee in her family roots for real.

"Come on over here sexy woman and let me see if you got any skills." I replied smiling back at her.

"Boy you don't know who your messing with." she said, flashing a pearly white smile, taking off the skin tight jeans she was wearing, then un-buttoning her silk shirt, revealing all her

Enemies Amongst Us	D. Isaac

beauty and a matching black bra and panty set. Standing there looking like a Victoria's Secrets model.

Looking at her standing there looking all sexy, sweet Willie jumped right to attention and I forgot all about gambling for a while. Baby-girl came over to me and helped me strip down to my boxers and started giving me a massage like she was a pro. All I could do is close my eyes and enjoy the moment.

After a few minutes of massaging me, she must've realized how hard sweet Willie was cause she said " why don't you put on a condom so I can see if you have any skills."

I didn't need any more encouragement than that. I jumped up and hurried to do her bidden.

Once I was strapped up, I finished undressing her removing her bra and panties but I told her to keep her heels on. Lisa had a sexy body like one of them chicks you see in one of them Smooth or king magazines. I could tell she took care of herself, spent time in the gym. Her ass was plump and firm, tits standing up by themselves and lil mama didn't have a single blemish or stretch mark on her body.

"Come on over here and kneel down on the couch facing the window." I told her.

Once I had her in that position, her face up against the window so she could look down and see the waves coming in form the Atlantic Ocean, I reached down and cupped both her breasts and started massing them making sure her nipples were hard.

"Ooooh yeah baby, I like that. That feels so good." She cooed.

Enemies Amongst Us   D. Isaac

As I was massaging her, I started sucking her neck and licking her ears making her body shiver with ecstasy. When she felt my hardness resting between the crack of her ass she arched her back and started gyrating her hips.

My hands went between her legs, her wetness soaked my fingers, and I knew she was ready. From the reflection in the window I saw her eyes were closed and she started wiggling her ass from side to side anticipating my next move.

I grabbed her butt, spread her cheeks and used my fingers to play with her.

"Yes baby, give me some." she moaned and wiggled against my fingers.

As I put my hardness up against her wetness, moving it up and down. feeling how wet she was. She cried out for me to stop teasing her.

Moving my hands to her waist, I slid into her inferno and started stroking her slow at first, squeezing her soft round ass, stroking, going deeper. I started hitting that pussy so hard she bumped her head into the window, still she didn't care she was loving every second of what i was doing to her.

"Don't stop, give it to me, fuck me hard, fuck me harder." she begged.

I started stroking her harder and faster. My balls started hitting her clit and I started slapping her on her ass. I reached around and held her by the shoulders. I was riding her hard like I was a cowboy on a race horse.

Enemies Amongst Us   D. Isaac

"Oh shit I'm cumming, I'm cumming." She screamed out and started bucking back, "Don't stop, Baby don't stop, keep it right there. Your hitting my spot." Lisa and I came at about the same time and as I eased out of her and turned around, I noticed Carlos standing behind us enjoying the show.

"My turn." He said coming over, picking her up and laying her on her back on the bed as I went to the bathroom to clean myself up for round two.

When I came out of the bathroom, Carlos had Lisa's legs on his shoulders, long stroking her. Carlos had baby girl moaning, groaning, and howling form deep within her throat. Watching them go at it turned me on so much, I eased over to the bed, so I could put my dick in Lisa's mouth while Carlos stroked her. I wanted in on the action. That's when my boy started hogging the pussy. He kept moving her head so I couldn't position her to get my dick in her mouth. The next thing I knew he started screaming.

"Who's pussy is this? Who's pussy is this?"

"Your's Carlos." she moaned, shaking her head like form side to side like she was having the time of her life.

I just stood there for a couple of minutes watching them, not believing my ears. We had just met these females downstairs less than an hour ago and now my boy was laying claim to her pussy like a stone cold sucker. To make matters worse she had the nerve to respond that it was his. I just got dressed and left the two of them there and went to the Black Jack tables to get my gamble on.

When I got back down to the tables my luck had changed and I went on a hot streak. About an hour later, I heard my name being

Enemies Amongst Us   D. Isaac

paged over the casino intercom. This had never happened to me before. All types of shit started going through my head. I started to panic, what if Carlos and them didn't pay the girls? What if the girls went and cried rape like what happened to Mike Tyson. I grabbed my chips from the table and started walking. Next thing I knew two security guards where coming in my direction. I turned around and started heading for the exit. When I got outside I turned around to see if they were still following me and there they were also coming through the exit doors. As I watched they just kept walking past me going about their business, not even paying me any mind. I was being paranoid. When I went back into the casino I ran into Rocky who'd been looking for me, and looked upset.

"What's going on?" I asked him.

"That blood-clat boy Carlos came to our room trying to fuck out girl too Starr." He said, pissed the fuck off.

That was Carlos, after he had finished with the girl I had left him with, he was still not satisfied. He still had to infringe on Rocky and Big Dreads fun as well.

Once I made sure everything was cool and the girls weren't tripping, and had got their money I went to the bar for a shot of Cristal and Alize. I need that thug passion to help me relax.

The following night while we was hanging out in the Casino floor we ran into Mike, the same dude from back in the days, that we'd try to set up with the two dummy keys.

"What's up Dread? How's things going with you?" He asked.

"Ain't nothing mike. Just chillin with a couple of my boys." I responded.

Enemies Amongst Us

D. Isaac

"What's up Carlos?" Mike asked.

"How you been Mike?" Carlos responded.

"Yo, I'm gonna play some more Black Jack before we leave." I explained, as I stepped off leaving Carlos and Mike talking.

It was about 11 PM when I was ready to hit the road and go home. Mike was hanging out in the room with Carlos when I came to get him and check out.

"Yo son, I'ma take Mike back to the city with us." Carlos said.

"What for?" I asked.

"He ain't got any place to stay, so I'ma let him crash with me for a couple days."

"That's on you son." I told him. This was typical Carlos. The man would bring home a stray dog from off the streets, always a soft heart. Here it was, he only had met mike twice in his life and he was willing to take him home with him, put a roof over his head, and he really didn't even know this dude.

After we were back in Brooklyn for a couple day Carlos called me and said he need to talk to me before he went back out of town. When he came and saw me he asked me to do him a favor and let Mike stay at my stash crib for a little while until he could find him a place to stay. I went against my better judgment and agreed to assist Carlos on his quest to saint hood and let Mike stay at my stash house.

After Mike was staying at my spot for a couple weeks, I noticed some of my things had started coming up missing. Then one day when I came into the building one of my neighbors, Renee, told me Mike had been bring crack head females around and partying all night with them while I wasn't there. He and his friends had the whole building smelling like a crack house at night from all the rocks they were smoking. After I'd heard that I told Mike he had to go and put him ass out. Unbeknown to me, the first thing Mike did upon me evicting him from my premises was call the FBI and tell them that I was committing all kinds of crimes. He told them a bunch of lies about how he was around me when I was planning murders and a bunch of robberies, when in fact I never did any such thing in his presence.

Chapter 23

Living in the concrete jungle known as New York City, your taught from a young age to always be aware of your surroundings. I had become a predator so I wouldn't be prey. Because of my lifestyle I was always on the look out for other predators trying to catch mc or my loved ones slipping. The lifestyle that I was living forced me to pay attention to any strange or out of the way things that was occurring around me. My paranoia has saved my life on many occasions.

    It was a beautiful sunny afternoon, I was feeling good about how things were going in my life when I decided to go and surprise Brittney at her job, and take her on a lunch date.

    As I was checking out all of the cars that were parked on the street where her office was located, I spotted my ex-wife Brenda

Enemies Amongst Us
D. Isaac

parked in her car down the street, stalking.

"Brenda what the hell do you think your doing?" I asked, approaching her car as she rolled down her window.

"I'm waiting for you bitch to come out so I can run her ass over." She said, as tears streamed down her face.

By the look on her face, and the sound of her words, I could tell that she was still hurting form our break up. It had never dawned on me that I had really hurt her like that. I realized that I needed to do something to calm her ass down before Brittney came outside, saw her, and all hell broke loose.

"Baby come in my car and let me talk to you for a couple of minutes." I told her.

When she got into my car, I drove around the corner and parked so Brittney wouldn't happen to walk by and get the wrong idea. Then I said to her.

"Brenda I'm really sorry for how things went down between us. I didn't mean to hurt or betray you. I wanted kids and you weren't giving me any, then this girl got pregnant and all I knew was I wanted this baby and shit escalated from there. Now how can I make this up to you? What do you want me to do?"

"There isn't anything you can do now about the baby Dee. I just loved you so much and for you to do this to me really hurts."

"Damn baby, I'm really sorry. Let me take you out to dinner this weekend so I can start making this up to you."

"Okay that's a start. I'll call you, but you know its gonna be a

Enemies Amongst Us — D. Isaac

long road if you want my forgiveness." She said, before I drove her back to her car and dropped her off.

Brenda called me the next day and told me that she wanted me to take her out Saturday evening. When I showed up at her house, lil mama came out looking sexy as the day we met wearing one of those short silk dresses showing off her exquisite legs. A lot of people say Brenda resembles Stephanie Mills, the only difference being that Brenda couldn't sing worth a damn. However she could blow real good like Karrine Stephens aka superhead and Brenda was also bow-legged like Nia Long.

Brenda wanted to go to a restaurant named The Cheese Cake Factory out in Roosevelt Fields on Long Island. We both ordered the sea-food platter, which consisted of lobster tails, scallops, fish fillet and baked potatoes. We shared a bottle of white Zinfandel wine with our food then had cheese cake with pineapple and strawberry toppings for dessert.

Our conversation was pleasant through out our evening together and we had a really good time talking about old times we shared together. I dropped Brenda back at her house at about 9 PM with a promise to do this again whenever she felt like it. Hoping that we could maintain a good friendship without any strings or old feeling getting in our way.

****

Brittney started acting like an old married couple months after she had delivered out baby. We was living together in a nice two bedroom apartment, and she must've felt like she had secured her position with me as my new wifey. I was doing everything to make her comfortable and happy, yet things still started to change drastically between us.

All random sex between us went right out of the window. No more getting head in the car, no more quickies during her lunch break or in the morning before she went to work. Also she stopped coming to bed wearing a t-shirt and thong and started wearing sweat pants. Then when I did get some pussy, it didn't feel the same as before she had the baby. It felt bigger to me for some reason. I wanted to take her ass back to the hospital so they could put a few more stitches on her vagina so it could be tighter like it was before. But I knew asking that would've meant world war three in my household.

I had asked a couple of my boys that had kids about this problem, and they all felt the same way after their women had delivered their kids too.

So just like the rest of the homies who weren't getting their freak on at home with their wives or baby mama's anymore because she was acting up. I started looking elsewhere to quench my aching appetite.

****

Chapter 24

I was out shopping for some mix tapes, or new CD's by Funk Master Flex, DJ Clue, and Kid Capri at this music store, on Fulton ST in downtown Brooklyn, when I made eye contact with this fine redbone cutie that looked like the young actress Lauren London. Shorty was cute as hell and was definitly checking me out. She had a pretty smile, and dimples just like Lauren. She was rocking some

Enemies Amongst Us   D. Isaac

skin tight blue daisy duke shorts behind the counter with a tank top that showed her flat stomach and belly button. When I saw how fat her monkey was through them shorts, I knew I had to have some of that.

"What's your name lil mama?" I asked, with a smile spitting my best game.

"Denise." she responded, flirting right back.

"You got a man Denise?" I asked, not wasting any time and cutting straight to the point.

"Nope, why you trying to be my man?" she asked, looking at me up and down from head to toe.

It just so happened to be one of those hot summer days and I was out chilling, so I was in floss mode. I had on a nice linen short set with some leather Clark sandal. Also I was blinged out rocking a new blue and black face Rolex with a diamond Bezel, I'd just bought from The Jewelry Exchange down in Philly. Not to mention I had a couple karats in my ears, bracelets, even a pinkie ring. My Italian link chain with the lions head piece had rubies in the eyes, and a big diamond in the mouth. All total, I probably had seventy grand worth of jewelry on. My trusted Glock 17 was in my waist fully loaded with a spare clip in my pocket to protect me from any haters or jack boys.

"Nah Ma,I Don't want to be your man. I already got a woman at home, but I would like to be your friends and lover." I told her, as I let my eyes slowly scan her from head to toe and back up again.

I was always up front with women about my relationship status

Enemies Amongst Us   D. Isaac

when I met them. This helped avoid any future problems, in case I ever bumped into them on the street with my woman, they would know their role and not say anything in front of wifey or disrespect her. A true playa knew how to keep his side chicks in the streets in line. So they would know to play their positions.

"You think you could handle being my friend and lover?" she asked, still smiling at me letting me know she appreciated my honesty.

"You better believe it sexy. I just want to make you happy and I know if I keep you happy you will keep me happy in return."

"Is that right! You think you got what it takes to keep me happy?" she responded obviously feeling me.

"You better believe it ma. I can do whatever it takes to make you happy. I'm quite capable of fulfilling all of your needs and wildest fantasies."

"What's your name?" She asked still eyeing me.

"My name is Dee, and what time do you get off work, so I can pick you up and take you to dinner?" This way I can spend some time with you and we can get to know each other better."

"I get off work at 6, and you better not leave me hanging." she replied looking deep into my eyes to express how serious she was.

"How da hell I'ma leave my new sexy lover hanging on our first date? Girl stop playing, here is my cell number so you can call me if I'm running late." I said, writing down the number and handing it to her.

Enemies Amongst Us   D. Isaac

Most New York girls were very aggressive, when they wanted something they went after it. That's one of the things I loved about my NY honnies. Denise had it and I had every intention on spending some time with her.

When I picked Denise up in front of her job in my Land Cruiser, I had on my boy Biggie's CD where he is rapping about having dreams of fucking an R&B chick pumping out of my system.

Once she was settled in her seat she said, "I'm starving where are you taking me to eat?"

"I know this little Italian joint in the city, I'ma take you there. Do you like Italian food?" I asked.

"Yeah, I like Italian food." she replied.

"Where do you live by the way?" I asked making small talk.

"I'm form uptown, I live in Harlem."

I took Denise to this restaurant named Luna's on Mulberry ST in little Italy in Manhattan. I was a regular there so always got A + service which always impresses ladies, plus the food was great.

"What would you like to eat?" I asked once we were seated.

"Why don't you order for the both of us, that's what a real gentleman would do." she said.

"I ordered a shot of Sambuca first for us, then the Shrimp Parmesan with spaghetti and marinara, and a carafe of the house red to wash down our meal with.

Enemies Amongst Us
D. Isaac

During dinner I found out Denise was a native New Yorker, and had lived in Harlem for all of her 28 years on this earth. She didn't have any kids, and had her own apartment. She had been in abusive relationship with a dude that was very insecure. She had only got out of it when dude had caught a murder beef and went to prison about a year before, and hadn't been with anyone since.

Denise lived in a big apartment building on the corner of Amsterdam AVE and 155th ST. This is the neighborhood that Dipset trap crew was from she had told me. There was no Jim Jones, Cam'ron or Juelz Santana around when we got here though.

When I pulled up in front of her building to drop her off she asked

"Do you wanna come up with me and chill for a little while? I had a good time tonight and don't want it to end yet."

"Sure, lil mama." I said then popped open my stash box and took out my Glock and extra clip. My gun was like my Visa I never left home without it.

She had a nicely furnished one bedroom apartment on the 10th floor, and once we were inside she told me to put some music on and make myself comfortable while she took a quick shower.

All she had was a bottle of Grand Marnier in her kitchen. I'd never tried it before but found it to be a very soothing Cognac.

When Denise came out of the shower she was wearing a big t-shirt. I had that 12 play Cd on by R. Kelly and "It seems like your ready" was coming out of her stereo. When she heard it she came over, sat in my lap and asked

Enemies Amongst Us — D. Isaac

"So you want to be my lover?" before she started kissing me.

I didn't get a chance to respond because her tongue was inside my mouth and I was enjoying the tingling sensation I was getting from her kisses and the Cognac.

I quickly found out that Denise was completely naked under the T-shirt, when I started massaging her soft round ass. Our kissing quickly grew intense.

"Just lay back and let me take care of you baby" she said as she slid out of my lap and knelt down in front of me and unzipped my pants.

Denise then took my erection in her mouth and started sucking and licking me until my toes curled up and my body started twitching from the reaction to all the caressing and licking she was doing. She used her warm mouth to suck my dick like she worshiped it, she sucked and licked me like she really loved and enjoyed what she was doing.

When I came she didn't stop either, she kept going until she had swallowed every drop of my liquid energy.

I was so turned on by her right then I would have given anything she asked for, but all she asked was

"You want to rest a minute before we go to the bedroom for part two?"

By the time I left Denise's apartment it was 4AM and I was completely exhausted. I could not remember being fucked and sucked like that for a long, long time.

Enemies Amongst Us   D. Isaac

I had a rule that when I was in the city creeping that I never let the sun come up before I was back at home with wifey. So although I wanted to stay with her, a playa had to respect the game and get up and take my ass home back to Brittney even if she was sleeping in her sweatpants.

As time went on kept spending with with Denise. i could not get enough of her. She was doing all kinds of freaky shit to me that both Brittney and Brenda had stopped doing. I was getting hooked on her like a dope fiend.

As time went by I started meeting some of Denise's friends while I was hanging out her. She asked me one day if I was into selling drugs. When I told her that I was not a drug dealer, and that I was into check and credit fraud she asked me to put her on the hustle so she could make some money also. She then introduce me to one of her girlfriends La-La.

La-La was a fine Puerto Rican girl that looked like Angie Martinez that worked for Hot 97 radio station in the city. La-La and Angie could pass for twins, they looked that much alike.

La-La also lived in Harlem went to the Borough of Manhattan Community College, and worked as a teller at a check cashing store in mid-town Manhattan.

I started giving La-LA an Denise credit cards to go shopping with. I also gave them, Brittney's and my sons sizes so when they went shopping for clothes they could pick up some things for my family as well. When income tax season came around I started giving LA-LA checks to cash for me at her job.

Chapter 25

Things had slowed down with my connects at the post offices, and it was getting hard for them to get credit cards during the fall season. The credit card companies were not sending as many cards during that time of year. I was only getting two or three cards per week without enough money on them to make them worth the risk.

Most credit card companies sent out credit cards and checks during the spring, summer and holiday seasons in an effort to get customers to spend money. It was during these times when some of the underpaid people working for the post office stole credit cards and checks. Income tax checks were another hot commodity during the spring time.

On days when I didn't have anything going on, I would hangout with Marilyn in her real-estate office and help her with customers who came by. Marilyn talked me into taking a real-estate course. I eventually passed the city exam and received my license as a sales agent.

I was hanging out at the office looking out of the window one day, when I noticed a dark skinned African looking dude pulling up in front of the building in a brand new gold Lexus GS300 with some fly chromed out rims. I had never seen this dude or his car before and I watched his movements as he exited the ride, and walked to the store. My money sensors started tingling and my brain started plotting.

When the dude entered the store, Marilyn got up form her desk and greeted him warmly, before calling me over.

Enemies Amongst Us   D. Isaac

"Hey Dee. I would like you to meet Yemi, he's from Africa. Yemi this is my dear friend Dee." she said introducing us.

"Bah-oh-nie." (what's up?) I greeted him in Ura-bah, a Nigerian dialect.

"Everything good." he responded, with a look of surprise that I spoke his language.

Yemi was a native of Nigeria, about 5'9" slim build with a shiny bald head. I could tell right away by his swagger that he was getting money, and I wanted some, if not all of it.

"Yemi, what can I do for you today?" Marilyn asked breaking my trance.

"I need a two bedroom apartment to rent Marilyn I have to move again, and I need you to run some info for me." He responded in a thick African accent while he skeptically looked around the store.

"You don't have to worry about Dee Yemi, he could probably help you out sometimes." Marilyn said, easing his discomfort.

"Oh yeah?" He asked, obviously curious.

"Come over here and let me run the info for you while you and Marilyn look for the apartment." I told him.

When Yemi sat down at my desk he pulled out about 50 credit cards, he needed information so he could activate them. As I ran the credit checks on the names that were on the cards, I engaged him in conversation trying to get a feel for him.

"Hey Yemi, I got people at ten radio shacks and three Nobody

Enemies Amongst Us   D. Isaac

Beats the Wiz stores that I don't need to show ID's, located right here around the city." I explained, setting the hook.

"For real?" He asked.

"Yeah I even got people in Atlantic City working in the casinos that do cash advances for me."

"Now your really talking my language Dee." He said, his excitement obviously building as he started grinning at me.

We exchanged numbers and made plans to get together the next day to do some business.

When we hooked up the following morning I was driving my Dodge Caravan and he was driving a Jeep Cherokee. We drove around the city for the entire day shopping at all the stores my connections worked at, even fueling up both vehicles with stolen credit cards. By the time we were though shopping it as late and this is when Yemi told me to follow him. He lead me to a storage facility located on Tilden Ave in Flatbush. He was renting this spot to stash his goods.

Over the next couple months I found myself hanging out with Yemi almost everyday. On some days he would call me over to his house and have me ride around town with him in one of his cars, while he met up with other Nigerians he did business with. I started to realize that he was trying to use me as a bodyguard, so I started to go along with it and play the roll.

He even asked me to go to an African Church service with him and his family one day. It turned out to be very colorful and enlightening for me. It's not that I had never went to church before. I was raised in the church when I was a youngster in Trinidad, and

Enemies Amongst Us   D. Isaac

even as an adult me and Brittney would attend services sometimes. It was just that I had never been to an African service where the entire congregation was Nigerians, including the pastor. All of the women were beautifully dressed in brightly colored traditional African clothing consisting of dresses and matching turbans. While some of the men wore traditional clothing most were immaculately dressed in the latest designer wear like Armani, Gucci, Cartier, and Mauri, and of course alligator shoes. The entire congregation was like a baller fashion show for African hustlers and their families.

When the preacher started asking for donations for his trip back to Africa, and said he wanted people that were going to donate more than a thousand dollars to step forward so he could say a special prayer for them I thought this service was a scam. But one by one they went up there more than I could count. After watching all them African ballers go up to the front of the church and watching the amount of money that basket collected, all I could think of was robbing the preacher. However being raised in the church I was to scared of God, and this is another line a good stick up kid never crosses.

While hanging out with Yemi one night he said to me.

"Hey Dee, I need you to drive down to Washington D.C. with me tonight."

"Oh yeah? What for?" I asked, wondering what he was up to.

"I got somebody down there that has over 100 cards they're trying to sell me." He explained.

"For real?" I asked, getting excited at the amount of money that could bring me.

Enemies Amongst Us   D. Isaac

"Yeah I need you to meet me at my house around midnight so we can drive down there and meet my connect first thing in the morning."

"Hey Yemi, how much money do I need to get some of those cards for myself?"

"Don't worry about that Dee, I got you."

"Alrght then I'll pick you up at 12 tonight" I said, driving off and thinking that he was gonna play fair with me and hook me with up some cards.

Later on that evening we jumped into his Lexus and hit the Turnpike heading south on I-95 all the way to our nations capital. Traffic was light at that hour so we rolled into D.C. about 3:30 AM and checked into the Washington Hilton Hotel on Dupont Circle.

When we got to our rooms I was not tired so I asked the bellhop, "Hey man what's up with the girls? I see hanging out on the corner? Can you bring one of them up here for me?"

"Man you don't want one of them things down there slim. Those are boys dressed up as girls." He explained with a smile as he shook his head.

"What da fuck!" I exclaimed, totally shocked. I had seen what appeared to be about 30 girls hanging around down on the corner now I was finding out that they were all men.

"For real slim, those are all dudes down there. They done took over the neighborhood and ran all the real girls across town to 14th and P. Things changed around here, This is where all of the rich Congressmen and Politicians come to indulge in their sick

Enemies Amongst Us   D. Isaac

fantasies with these boys and they be paying them a lot of money."

My bellhop was a very cool older cat, a Native Washingtonian. After talking with him I gave him a $50 tip, told him good looking out, and locked my door.

Since I was up and couldn't sleep, I decided to give my boy KG a call and see what he was into. I had met KG a couple years back while I was down here in DC hanging at this club called the Mirage. Carlos had introduced us KG's real name was Kevin Gray and he had DC on lock. He was a major player in the DC/Baltimore area. If you were not buying drugs or working for him your ass was in trouble if him or his crew found out about it. Most likely your ass would end up robbed and murdered for violating their turf. Real iron fist, dictator type dude.

"What up Kev?" I asked, when he picked up his phone.

"Who this Dex?" He asked, to make sure it was me.

"Yeah nigga it's me and I'm down here in your city."

"What's up slim? What brings you to my zip code?" He asked.

"I came down here to handle some business with one of my African homies." I explained.

"Oh yeah? Ya'll better not be trying to open up shop in my city, I know how ya'll NY niggas do. Remember what we did to the last NY niggas that came down here un-invited." He said, as he laughed into the phone.

"You ain't gotta worry about us setting up shop, we just down here for a couple hours to grab something then we're gone in the morning. I couldn't sleep so I figured I'd give you a call and see what you were up to."

"I'm chilling at the Ritz club. It's packed with some fine ass women if you wanna come hang out for a few.

"Hell yeah. I'm wide awake and need something to do."

"Do you want to come meet me or do you want me to pick you up? Where you staying at anyway?"

I still had the keys to Yemi's Lexus, but as I thought about driving to meet him, I changed my mind because I knew it was not wise to be riding around in DC late at night with NY license plates on a new car, especially unarmed.

"I'm at the Washington Hilton Hotel on DuPont Circle." I explained.

"What da hell are you doing over there with them fags Slim? You ain't changed up on me have you?" KG joked, as he cracked up laughing.

"Hell no son, I love women to much, I think they're the greatest thing God ever created." I retorted.

"A'ight just making sure, this is the spot for you if you like females. I'll be there in a few minutes wait outside for me." he said ending the call.

KG pulled up in front of the hotel 10 minutes later pushing a brand new black S500 Mercedes Benz, and tailed by a green Chevy Tahoe with four females in it.

When I climbed into his Benz he said, "It's good to see you

Enemies Amongst Us   D. Isaac

Dex, I brought some of my home girls to hang out with us. I'ma take you to one of DC's go-go joints so you can see how we do it in the Nations Capital."

"A'ight let's do this." I said with a smile, glad to be out of the hotel room.

KG took me to this spot call Club that was located right on U street, down the street from Ben's Chili Bowl. It was kinda dead due to the late hour so we only stayed for a couple drinks before I asked him to take me back.

When he dropped me back at the hotel we made plans to go to the go-go again the next time I came to DC, so I could get an early taste of all the action.

When I got back to the hotel room all I had time for was a quick shower before Yemi had me back in the car driving him through the neighborhood known as Georgetown to meet up with his card connect.

Yemi's connect turned out to be a bald headed short Nigerian dude who seemed extremely nervous when he got into the car with us. While sitting there watching Yemi make the transaction, I realized that my boy was really on top of his game. He bought 150 cards for $10,000. After verifying that every last one of them had at least $2,500 on them he pulled out the 10 grand to pay his connect and we headed straight back to the highway for our four hour trip back home.

When we got back to Brooklyn, Yemi told me to go straight back to his apartment in Flatbush. As soon as I pulled the car into his garage he jumped out, ran around to the trunk of the car, pulled

Enemies Amongst Us
D. Isaac

out the credit cards, and started going through them.

Here you go Dee, just give me $200 for these." He said handing me two cards with only $2,500 limit each,

"What's this Yemi?" I asked him, trying my best to keep from slapping the shit out of him and taking all the cards from his bitch ass right then and there.

"I can only spare these two cards. I need the rest to do something." He replied in his thick African accent, pissing me off even further.

"Yemi, before we left I told you that I needed to buy some cards for myself also."

"I know Dee that's why I'm selling you two of them. I need the rest to take care of my people." He explained.

From being around Yemi over the last couple of months, I had come to the realization that he was a selfish mutha fucka, and he liked to use people. After this conversation with him, and how he was trying to play me like a sucker, I came to the conclusion that I was going to back a cake for his bitch ass real soon. I was going to rob the shit out of him and take all his shit. About a week later I was chilling at the real-estate office with Marilyn, when I realized I hadn't seen her husband around lately.

"Hey Marilyn, where is Habib, why ain't he been around lately?" I asked her, thinking that it had to have been at least a couple of months since I'd seen him.

"His name is Sayeed not Habib Dee, and I don't want to talk about him." she said, getting an attitude.

Enemies Amongst Us   D. Isaac

I knew something was wrong right there cause Marilyn never let anyone know when something was bothering her. She played her cards very close to her vest and kept her feelings to herself.

"What's wrong baby girl? What that bastard do to you?" I asked, genuinely concerned.

"Dee, after all I did for him, you'd never believe what he told me."

"What'd he say baby girl?" I asked her realizing she really wanted to talk about this.

"Dee ,after I married him, he got his green card and could be here legally. Now he wants to tell me that he can't be with me cause I'm not a true Muslim."

"What the fuck?" I screamed out.

"Yeah Dee, that's what I said too." she agreed then added "He moved out of my house about two months ago and got his own place. Now he's bragging about bringing his Muslim wife over here from his country. He wants a divorce and half of all the properties I own and money I have saved."

"Marilyn didn't I see you wearing Muslim clothes when you first started bringing him around?" I commented, not knowing what else to say.

"Yeah Dee, I had converted to Islam form my Christian faith to please him. The mutha fucka even had me praying five times a day, and now he pulls this shit?" she said, with a sob and began wiping her eyes.

Enemies Amongst Us
D. Isaac

I knew Marilyn was really upset not only because I had never heard her use profanity before, but I'd also never seen her cry. My friend was hurting and now I was getting angry with Sayeeds bitch ass because he had done this to to a good person. I really didn't want to get involved in her domestic issues this type of shit can easily flip on a brother. I had to give it some strong thought instead of just acting on the feelings from what she shared caused.

After I finished consoling Marilyn, I got the address of the house Yemi had rented from her. He must've forgotten that I knew about it. Later on that evening I drove out to the address to begin my surveillance of his new residence.

Chapter 26

Yemi lived on the first floor of a two story house located on a nice quite residential street in Carnasie. I had been plotting on him for about three days when I got a call from my boy Pierre.

"What's good Dex?" He asked, when I answered my phone.

"Ai'nt nothing Pierre." I responded then continued "What's good with you?"

"Dex, I want to come up to the city to visit with you for a couple of days. Is that cool with you?" He asked.

"Of course my man, you know your like family so it's all good."

"Speaking of family Dex, is it ok if I bring my cousin Rick with me?"

"Sure Pierre, Rick is cool, bring him along it's no problem." I told him.

He had introduced me to Rick down in Atlantic city a while back and he seemed like a laid back dude, so I didn't have a problem with them coming up and staying at my crib for a couple days.

"Alright then Dex, we'll see you in a couple of hours." He said, before hanging up.

Later on that night while me and a couple of my boys were waiting on Yemi to come home, so we could run up on him

Enemies Amongst Us

D. Isaac

Brittney hit me up on my cell.

"Hey Baby what are you doing?" she asked, when I answered.

"Just kicking it with the fellas." I responded. I never let Brittney know what was going on in the streets. I did my best to keep my home and street life completely separate.

"Your boy Pierre, and another dude are here looking for you." she said.

"Oh shit, baby let them in I'll be there in a few minutes, I completely forgot. I told them they could stay with us for a couple days while they in the city."

"Alright baby I'll see you when you get here." she said, as we disconnected our call.

"Aye yo! I got to shoot to my crib for a couple of minutes." I explained to Mugsy and Carlos, who were in the car on the stake out with me.

When we got to my house Pierre introduce Rick to everybody and we sat around and kicked it for a little while. After a few minutes of small talk Pierre asked.

"Hey Dee, what was y'all doing before we got here?"

"Actually we was handling some business we have to get back and finish." I told him then finished "I'll be back in a couple of hours."

"Dee, we didn't drive two hours just to come sit in your house. We came up here to see what New York is all about." He whined.

Enemies Amongst Us   D. Isaac

"Pierre, what we're going to do is dangerous and I don't want to put your lives at risk." I started then added " Listen you can either chill out here with Brittney or ya'll can come with us." Once I'd seen clouds of disappointment coming over their expressions.

"You sure you want to roll with the Big Dogs?" I asked, laughing as I messed with him.

"Yeah Dee, lets roll." He replied.

When we went outside we all walked over to my car where I gave Mugsy and Carlos their set of walkie talkies. They already had their guns and fake police badges on them.

That was when Pierre realized I had on a bullet proof vest and him and Rick were the only ones without guns.

"Aye Dee, you got guns for us to?" He asked shyly.

"Yeah I got guns for you but your not gonna need me. Ya'll just gonna chill out in the van with me and keep an eye out for the police." I explained knowing damn well I was not about to let Pierre and Rick participate in the robbery. Pierre was a upstanding dude with a 9 to 5 job, a real citizen, not a street thug. He was just fascinated by the thug lifestyle and wanted a little action in his life, after all that's why he came up to the Big Apple for a couple of days.

After staking out Yemi's crib for a couple of hours, I decided to call it a night on this Jux and treat Pierre and Rick to a night at one of Brooklyn's raunchiest strip clubs. I had just the place in mind. Club 88, located on Foster Ave. right behind The Brooklyn's Terminal Market, in Carnasie.

Enemies Amongst Us			D. Isaac

After a couple hours at the strip club, we decided to call it a night and head back to my house for some rest.

I awoke to the smell of turkey sausage and pancakes. Brittney was cooking in the kitchen early in the morning. My wifey was being a good hostess and preparing breakfast for me and my friends. Afterwards Brittney left to go drop our son off at the babysitter so she could go to work.

It was about 10 AM when I hit the streets with Pierre and Rick in my van. I was ready to give them a tour of the badest borough in the city of New York, more commonly known as Crooklyn.

Pierre wanted to do a little shopping while they were here so my first stop was to take them to Kings Plaza Mall, located in Mill Basin. This was a predominately white neighborhood in the early 70's and 80's. When I first arrived in America in 1975 and was transferred to Roy H. Mann Junior High School. There was no African Americans living in the neighborhood.

Now by the mid 90's things had changed drastically. Black people now dominated this area. A lot of families were migrating form the West Indies, buying homes in this area, and pushing the whites out to Long Island.

After Pierre and Rick had bought a few outfits from the mall I took them to Flatbush so they could see the different clothing stores on Flatbush Ave.

As we cruised around checking out the stores I received a hit on my pager. When I called the number back it was this dude Curtis that I'd bought credit cards from sometimes.

"What's up rude boy?" I asked, when he answered the phone.

Enemies Amongst Us   D. Isaac

"I need to see you Dread, I got something you might be interested in." He said without any preamble, but plenty of excitement ringing through his vocal cords.

"Oh yeah?" I asked, picking up on his excitement, then added "What you got? Curtis only called me when there was money to be made so needless to say I loved his calls. Ours was a good solid business relationship, everyone comes up, everyone wins.

"I got some paper I need to show you, but I can't talk about it one the phone. When can we hook up so you can see this with your own eyes?"

Never one to sleep on a deal that could pay my pocket I replied.

"Where you at right now?"

"I'm in the Bronx right now but I'll be in Crooklyn in a couple of hours if you wanna meet up then." He said, taking a shot at my borough.

"Alright, for sure, hit me up when you get back, and we'll figure out where to meet at." I said ending the call.

"Aye yo Dex, I want one of those motorcycle jackets everybody is rocking." Pierre said, when I got off the phone.

"Pierre, you don't even have a motorcycle what the fuck do you want the jacket for?" I asked him.

"They look nice." He said with a smile then added " I see a lot of dudes up here wearing them, and ain't nobody in Atlantic City rocking them yet. I wanna be the first."

"You know those jackets cost about a grand right?" You got that

Enemies Amongst Us					D. Isaac

kind of money?"

"Nah Dee, I ain't got that much but you could get it for me and I'll make it up to you somehow when you come down to the casino." He offered, looking at me like a little kid. I was starting to feel like a big brother to Pierre, next thing you know I'd be claiming him on my taxes. What can I say I had a soft spot for the dude, so I took him over to 5th Ave. in the city and bought him a Vanson leather jacket for $900. On our way back to Brooklyn Curtis hit me on the cell again.

"Aye yo Dread, I'm back in BK where you wanna do this?"

"Yo. meet me in front of Apaches in 15 minutes." I told, him ending the call.

Apache was a Jamaican dude who operated a restaurant located on Prospect Place between Nostrand Ave and Rodgers Ave. right in the heart of Crown Heights.

He specialized in escovitch fish and festival bread. His restaurant had the best fish and fresh bread in all of Brooklyn. This fact was proven by the line that was always in front of his spot. It was a true Brooklyn landmark for West Indian Food.

Besides the food Apache had five of his beautiful daughters working the counters and dudes showed up just to flirt with them. I mean who doesn't enjoy dinner with a view?

When I pulled up in front of Apache's Curtis was already parked on the block sitting in his blue S500 Mercedes Benz. He waved when he saw my van pull up, then locked his car and hopped in the back with Rick.

"Curtis these are my boys Pierre and Rick." I said, greeting him and introducing them.

"What's up?" He asked, giving them both dapps then added "Nice to meet you boys."

"A'ight Curtis, what you got for me?" I said, cutting him off and getting right down to business.

"Dread I got some people making these." He said, pulling out an envelope, full of money, from inside his leather coat, and handing it to me.

"Damn Curtis." I said, as I fingered the bills "You done hit the jackpot with these." I continued as I passed some of the loot to Pierre and Rick.

The envelope contained an assortment of 100's, 50's, and 20's all very professional counterfeits.

"Yo Curtis, how much this shit going for?" I asked him as my eyes rolled around like a slot machine about to land on 7 7 7

"Dread, for you man I can go down to 35 cent on the dollar for as much as you want." He replied, his voice was music to my ears.

"Yo Pierre, we on the same page right now?" I asked, already knowing what his greedy ass would say.

"Yeah Dee, get some I can handle this." He replied, beaming with excitement.

"How much you want me to get?" I said, letting him make the call.

Enemies Amongst Us					D. Isaac

"Get about twenty g's to start, and we'll see how that goes."

"Yo Curtis, how long is it going to take you to get 20 grand of these for me?" I asked, as all types of thoughts started running through my head. All of which had something to do with different ways to flip these counterfeit bills. Everything form buying Kilo's of cocaine from the Dominicans and Colombians to having Pierre switch some out. The potential was great.

"I can have them for you in a couple of hours. All I have to do is go back to the Bronx to pick it up. 20 g's worth is gonna cost you seven in real bread Dread. How long you gonna need to put that together?" He asked, me trying to get everyone on the same page.

"Soon as your ready, I'll be ready homie." I let him know hoping it would light a fire under his ass to get this ball moving.

"A'ight that's why I like fucking with you Dread. Let me go handle my business and I'll call you back and tell you where to meet me at." He said before he exited the van.

Once he's left I asked Pierre and Rick,

"Ya'll sure you can handle this business?"

"Yeah Dee, we got this. All I got to do is mix them with the real money when I'm working the cage." Rick said, then Pierre added.

"The real concern is how much are you going to give us for doing this?"

"I'll tell ya'll what I'm gonna do. It's costing me an investment of seven grand for this stuff. Ya'll just double me up, giving me fourteen, and keep the other six for yourselves. How's that sound?"

I said, breaking it down for them.

   They looked at each other, smiled, then looked at me and both said, "That's a deal Dee."

   "Aigh't good, now let me treat you Yankee Boys to some real West Indian cooking before we go pick up the paper form my boy." I said, as we exited the vehicle.

   Later on that night we met up with Curtis in the parking lot of McDonald's restaurant right off the belt parkway in Queens, near Farmer Blvd. I gave Curtis the seven grand and he gave me the 20 g's of counterfeit money. After the transaction was done we began the drive back to my house in Carnasie.

When we got back inside my apartment and I showed Pierre and Rick the bag with all the fake 100's and 50's in it, they hit the ceiling. The first thing out of Pierre's mouth was,

   "Yo, Dee I'm ready to get on the highway to go back home right now. I wanna take care of this business."

   I looked at my rolly and realized it was already midnight and I could tell by Pierre's and Rick's demeanor that they were really excited about making some money. However since it was already late and we'd been running the streets all day I replied,

   "Ain't no need to rush, Y'all just get some rest and you can leave first thing in the morning."

   "Alirght then, that's what we'll do." They both agreed and we all called it a night.

   A few days after Pierre and Rick went back to Atlantic City I

Enemies Amongst Us
D. Isaac

had Carlos and Mugsy run up on Yemi as he was going into his house. It was about 11 PM and I stayed in my car and kept look out for police, mainly because i didn't want Yemi to recognize me and cause any problems for Marilyn. Carlos told me once they were inside Yemi's crib they duct taped him and his wife and started questioning him about where his stash was. He held his ground and like any money hungry, respectable hustler, he didn't want to give up his paper that easy. Thus forcing Mugsy to resort to drastic measures, he grabbed their two year old infant son and threatened to drown him in their bath tub. When Yemi's wife seen Mugsy submerging her little baby in the water, she shouted that the money was in the padding of their living room sofa.

    Carlos and Mugsy left Yemi's house with 90,000 in cash, about 70,000 in jewelry, 80 new credit cards, and 8 large trash bags filled with all kinds of women's designer clothes. Everything from Versace, Gucci, Prada, Chanel, Armani, all the way down to Hugo Boss. They loaded all the goods into his GS300 Lexus and followed me to my stash house so we could split up the loot. We took the Lexus to send a message that we wanted it all, everything he had. However we ended up finding a chop shop in Red Hook that gave us eight g's for it. Sometimes when you play well your rewarded.

    Yemi lost all of his shit cause his bitch ass didn't want to play fair with me. That's what suckers get when they don't respect the game. The following week I went down to Atlantic City to do some cash advances and give Pierre a couple of Yemi's old suits. I couldn't sell them and figured I'd use them to keep my man in A.C. pleased.

Chapter 27

Things were going good for me and my crew after we had robbed Yemi. Everybody was busy getting money doing something. Carlos was going back and forth carrying drugs from Washington DC to NYC. He was going up and down the highway almost every week. He had bought a Honda accord with some of his cut from the robbery, and had a bike rack installed on the roof of it. He would then stuff the inside of the bicycle tire with crack cocaine, and heroin and mount the bikes on the roof of the car. When the cops on patrol saw his car going down the highway they never paid him any attention or suspected him for a drug trafficker. At a quick look he would just appear to be a regular clean cut guy that was probably a professional bicycle rider. Whatever they thought it worked cause he was never stopped, not even once.

Carlos started making so much money carrying drugs down to the Nations Capital that he went and put a down payment on a 3 bedroom, one family house in DC. Like most smart drug dealers he put it in his girlfriends name. He then brought his brother down there to do some renovations on it for him and had the house looking brand new in no time at all.

Carlos had a head for business. After he sold his drugs down in DC, he would then buy a lot of stolen merchandise from the drug addicts, and other hustlers, and bring it back to New York to re-sell it. That way he made money on each leg of his trip, thus maximizing his profits. The living room at his mothers house looked like a little Wal-Mart. He had it filled with computers, radios, televisions, name brand pocket books, male and female clothes, and even a few guns stashed about. My boy was doing his thing and I was proud of him. The only thing I didn't like was when he'd buy the cocaine he would bring it to his mother's house and cook it up into crack in her basement.

My boy was getting money, but he was violating the hustlers rule book by being cheap and not renting a place to do his dirt at. A true playa would not put his loved ones at risk like this. I tried talking to him about this but he was hard headed and set in his ways, plus his mother and father were old school gangsters, so they didn't mind what he did as long as he broke them off with some paper in the end. It was all good.

****

Mugsy took some of his money from the jux and went and leased a big ass white 400 SEL Mercedes Benz. He also put some money down on a 3 bedroom town house out by Kennedy Airport in Queens for his wife and 5 kids.

Mugs had hooked up with another crew from Flatbush, that was into picking locks and burglarizing houses. So on most day he was just riding around town flossing and picking up chicks while he waited for someone to call him with a new jux.

****

My boy Black was still into doing robberies. Whenever things were slow for him he would come around, and when I bought credit cards I would always sell him a couple of them so he could eat also. Spreading love was the Brooklyn way, and I lived by it.

Enemies Amongst Us   D. Isaac

I knew Black was not doing well, but he was surviving. He was not coming around with his hands out wanting somebody to give him something. The brother was willing to get down for his. He had proven that to me through out the time I had spent with him.

They say the freaks come out at night but that could be debatable. During summer time in New York City, the freaks are out 24/7 parading the streets half naked during the day time as well as the nights, because of the heat and humidity in the atmosphere. Beautiful women of all colors, shapes and sizes could be found everywhere.

It was on one of these day as I was riding around town with Black, in my Toyota Land Cruiser, bored with nothing to do, when I got a call from this chick named Angie from Clinton Hills.

"What's up Dee? What are you doing?" she asked, when I answered my cell.

"Chillin rollin around with one of my boys." I responded.

"Dee, I need to make some money." she asked. Angie was one of the girls I had shopping for me with the credit cards, plus she was one of my sex buddies. The only time she ever called me, was when she needed some money and she was always down to do whatever to earn it.

"I ain't got any work right now baby girl. Where you at though?" I asked her, euphorically recalling her A+ head game and suddenly becoming in the mood for some.

"Dee, I need two hundred dollars to take care of something, and

Enemies Amongst Us				D. Isaac

I'm at my crib. What's up you coming through?" she asked.

"Yeah, I'm coming over, but I got one of my boys with me and I want you to hook him up."

"Oh yeah? He got some money?"

"I got him. He's my peoples and he is a little stressed out right now, so I want you to look out for him."

"A'ight then, I'll see you when you get here. How long you gonna be?"

"I'll be there in 15 minutes baby." I said, hanging up the phone.

"Yo Black, today is your lucky day. I'm about to treat you to some good ass pussy from one of my shorties." I told him with a smile.

"For real Dee?" He asked, smiling back at me.

"For real son, I got you. Just follow my lead when we get to her crib."

Angie was about 5'5" with a chocolate complexion. She wore her hair short like Halle Berry, and had some nice big tits on her short frame. She was shaped like the actress Taraji P Henson, all tits and no ass. But lil mama had skills in the bedroom that could give Heather Hunter, Janet Jacme or Pinky a run for their money.

When Angie answered her door, all she had on was a t-shirt and a yellow thong. Black's jaw almost hit the ground when he saw her standing there looking sexy as hell and shiny and glowing from the coconut oil she was wearing all over her body.

Enemies Amongst Us   D. Isaac

Once seated in Angie's living room and after introductions were made I asked, "Yo Black, you want to go first?"

"Nah Dee, you go first." He said, looking a little nervous.

"What's wrong son? You getting all shy on me all of the sudden?" I asked.

"Leave him alone Dee, and come back here with me." Angie said getting up and leading the way to her bedroom.

When Angie left I said, "Yo, son this is what we are going to do, when we go into her bedroom I"ma tell her to give me some head, and that your gonna hit her form behind while she is giving me head. You cool with that?"

"Yeah lets go." Black said, enthusiastically.

When we went to Angies bedroom, I put my gun down on her dresser, took off my pants, and boxers, then got into bed and started playing with her breasts.

"Oooh yeah Oooo yeah." she moaned enjoying the way I was massaging her.

"You wan some of this long dick?" I asked, her talking dirty cause I knew that was one of her major turn ons.

"Yeah baby please, you know I want some." she responded.

"Take off your panties so my boy can hit that pussy from behind while you suck this dick then." I told her.

"Okay baby, but let me make sure he puts on a condom first." she agreed.

Enemies Amongst Us

D. Isaac

After she passed Black a condom, Angie started doing her thing, and doing it well. Baby girl was deep throating my dick like it was her favorite flavor of popsicle on a scorching hot day. I was in heaven. She had that ass cocked up in the air and spread wide open waiting, longing for Black to have his way.

After a few minutes, I realized that Black wasn't doing anything to her. He just kept fumbling with himself. "What the fuck you doing son?" I finally asked.

"My joint won't get hard." He cried.

"What?" I asked, in disbelief.

"My joint won't get hard" He repeated himself sounding like a whiney little kid.

Me and Angie both looked at each other like we couldn't believe this shit.

"A'ight son lets switch positions, let me get back there and show you how to fuck that pussy." I said, getting up and putting on a rough rider condom.

I like getting head in the raw, but I was not into fucking any of my shorties without protection. I didn't care how good they looked or how good the pussy was. I had to strap up my shit. I couldn't take any risks, taking some shit home and giving it to wifey. Like most men I didn't feel like I could catch a disease just form getting head.

Angie's pussy felt like it was on fire when I entered her and started hitting her with the long stroke I knew she loved. "Who's pussy is this?" I asked her, while she had Black's dick in her

Enemies Amongst Us — D. Isaac

mouth.

"Your's daddy." she replied, spitting out Black's joint. then added "Something is wrong with you boy Dee, his shit still ain't getting hard."

"What?" I couldn't believe this shit. "Yo Black, why don't you go wait for me in the living room while I finish handling my business back here." I told him.

Black was embarrassing the shit out of me. I felt like he was making me look bad by not representing in front of one of my chicks. This dude be running up in peoples houses and robbing them, but he was nervous around this chick for some reason.

After I finished with Angie I just layed there with her for a couple of minutes and thought about Black and this situation. He had me starting to wonder if his ass was gay or something. He could be one of those homo thugs running around like a gangster but is on dick or ass on the down low. As I was laying there thinking, I remembered that he had told me a while back that he had a girlfriend, but the more I thought about it, I started to realize that I had never seen him with her or any other females. I said to myself that I might have to start paying more attention to his ass from now on.

****

A couple days after the episode with Angie, Black called me while I was at the real estate office with Marilyn "Yo Dee, I need to talk to you right away where you at?" He asked.

"I'm at the real estate office, what's up?" I responded.

"I'll be right there." He said, hanging up the phone.

About 15 minutes later he showed up at the office all excited "What's up playa?" I asked, him after he was seated.

"Dee, I got me some credit cards and I need you to get the info on them for me so I can activate them." He said, all excited pulling 8 new credit cards out of his pants pocket and placing them on the desk in front of me.

"Slow down playboy, where did you get these cards from?" I asked. I knew Black always got his cards from me and didn't have a postal connection so the whole situation set off my radar.

"Dee, I got me a connect now, and I just bought these from her." He countered, still pushing the issue.

"Oh yeah? Who is she?" I asked. Still skeptical.

"Dee, I can't tell you who she is. You know who she is and she knows who you are, but you don't know that she works for the post office. If I tell you then you might go and cut my throat."

"It's all good then playa, I don't need to cut your throat. You keep your connect for yourself."

Black started getting his own cards regularly form his new connect and was starting to stack up his paper. I was proud of his success, as I've never been one to hate on my friends progress. I liked to see all my boys do good and get money. There was enough money for all of us out there, we just had to be ambitious enough to go get it.

About a month later Black started to have some trouble with his

Enemies Amongst Us — D. Isaac

car, so he came to me on day and asked "Yo Dee, why don't you sell me that Stanza sitting out front of your house? Your girl don't be driving it anyway."

Ever since I had bought Brittney her C280 Mercedes Benz, she had stopped driving the Stanza, and just left it sitting in front of the house. She didn't even move it to the right side of the street in the mornings before she went to work so the sanitation people could clean the street when they came through. The ticket people were having a field day piling up tickets on her car. Seemed like every night I came home there was a new ticket on it, I was honestly surprised they hadn't "booted" it yet.

"Alright Black, just give me $5,000 and the car is yours."

"Yo Dee, can I use the plates until I can get the car registered in my name?"

"Yeah you could do that, but I need my plates back in two weeks."

"Okay, you got that and I appreciate you." He agrees I would later find out that Blacks's credit card connect was my boy from back in the day, Buddy's, sister Tanya. Tanya ended up getting busted by the postal police and made a deal to set up Black so she could avoid prosecution, prison and keep her kids. She called Black one day, while she was wearing a wire, pretending to sell him some cards. Black went to meet up with her driving the Stanza that was still registered in my name. Tanya then had Black count the money out loud for her in the car, while recording the whole thing. Once he had finished counting the five hundred measly dollars the postal police surrounded the car and locked his dumb ass up.

Enemies Amongst Us   D. Isaac

    Instead of keeping his mouth shut and handling his own problems like a real man, Black decided to become a rat and save himself. He became the next "Sammy the Bull", a government informant, to avoid prison. So now unknowingly, I was riding around with a government informant that was pretending to be my friend, when in reality he was plotting my downfall. I had an enemy amongst me and I didn't even know it.

Chapter 28

I was at the real estate office with Marilyn and Black. We were Running some credit checks on some names from some cards Black and I had just bought when Marilyn said " Hey Dee, I'm ready to sell this real estate business are you interested in buying it?"

"Sure Marilyn, but what's going on with you that makes you want to sell it all of the sudden"? I replied, knowing how much work she had put into that business to build it from the ground up.

"Dee, remember the last time we talked about Sayeed? Well since then he has filed for divorce from me and he keeps calling and threatening to take half of my money and properties. So before I let that happen, I'm going to sell everything before the divorce goes through and leave the country with my hard earned money"

"Damn girl, he really trying to jack you for half your paper huh? God bless America."

"Yeah Dee, that Arab mutha fucka thinks he is going to take my shit and give it to his Arab bitch , but I got a trick for his ass. He ain't going to get one damn penny from me." she said, her anger rising with every word.

"Marilyn I thought he had his own money? Don't tell me you went and married a broke ass Arab mutha fucka?"

"He got a little something Dee, he ain't completely broke, but he ain't rich either. He been saving up all his money."

Enemies Amongst Us
D. Isaac

"About how much money you think he got?" I asked, her automatically focusing in on how to make his money my money. Hey, living in Brooklyn's expensive.

"Well. I know he keep about 40-50 grand in cash when he lived with me. He don't believe in keeping his money in the bank. He and one of his friends bought one of those yellow taxi cabs, and they be taking turns driving it, so he has cash on him everyday."

"Marilyn, you know where he's living at?" I asked her, looking at Black to see if he was picking up on the direction this was heading.

"Yeah Dee. Why would you want to know though? What you thinking in that big head of yours?"

"I'm thinking about robbing his bitch ass and teaching him a lesson for fucking with you."

"Dee, if you do that, you got to be careful. remember when you first met him, you thought he was a terrorist?"

"Yeah, I remember telling you he looked sneaky."

"Well you should've listened to your instincts."

"What're you trying to say Marilyn?"

'Do you remember when they tried to blow up the world trade center, with that bomb in the van?"

"Yeah I do." I replied, thinking back to that cup of coffee with LA in Cayuga Correctional, as CNN broke the whole story.

"Well, Sayeed told me that one of the people that was in the

Enemies Amongst Us   D. Isaac

van was his cousin. The night before they did that he had some of his friend over at my house, they had cooked up a lamb, and were talking about how they have to sink the fear into the American Infidel dogs."

"Damn girl, why didn't you tell me all this shit before?"

"I didn't know at the time what they were talking about Dee. Most of the time they were speaking Arabic. Besides he was my husband, and I thought he was in love with me like I was with him."

"Did you tell anybody else about this? Did you go to the cops?"

"No Dee, like I said I was in love with him he was my husband."

"Damn Marilyn, we got enemies amongst us right here in Brooklyn, and we don't even know it."

"So what are you gonna do now Dee? You still want to rob him and kick his ass for me?"

"Your damn right! I'm gonna do it. I had some good friends that worked in that building. Carlo's father worked there, my friend Ivan worked over there, even my friend Ray and his wife Dawn both worked in that building." I said building up momentum then finishing "So hell yeah, I'm gonna kick his ass and rob the little Arab fucka. Baby girl, I was raised in these Brooklyn streets and we ain't scared of any god damn camel riding Arab terrorist. Honestly if you ask me his rent is over due anyway." I told her knowing Sayeed's ass was in trouble when I caught up to him.

"Now getting back on track" I said, never being one to pass up

Enemies Amongst Us   D. Isaac

a opportunity to make some money "How much did you want for this real-estate business?"

    She smiled at me completely not surprised, as I steered the conversation right back to where we left off "Dee I was going to ask $20,000 but since your my friend I'll come down to $10,00 for you. Especially considering your going to kick Sayeed's ass for me.

    She was half right, I was going to kick Sayeeds ass, but it was more for my benefit than hers, believe that!

    "Yo, Dee, let me go half with you on that and I'll go half on the ass kicking to." Black butted in with a laugh.

    Now Black was one of my crime partners, we was cool as far as doing short term crime together. Investing in a legitimate business was another ball game, and I didn't know if I was ready for that type of commitment with him. When you go into business with someone you have to be able to make comprises, and I liked to do things my way so this was something I needed to seriously contemplate before I committed myself or my funds.

    "Yo Black, let me think about that and I'll get back to you." I told him.

    "Nah Dee, you just tryna spin me and leave me out." He said, not letting it go.

    "Listen Black, I'ma keep it real with you son, I'm thinking about getting out the Game soon and going legit."

    "Yo Dee, I feel you on that, and I'm trying to do the same, that's why I'm trying to get my paper up."

Enemies Amongst Us   D. Isaac

"Man Black I have been thinking about going legit ever since Brittney had my son I got responsibilities now, I'm not just living for myself anymore. I got a family now and I got to start thinking about them, so I'm ready to leave all this street shit alone and invest in some legitimate business and chill the fuck out. I got a couple more things lined up then I'm out for real son, word to mutha."

"So your serious, huh Dee?"

"Hell yeah I'm serious, and if your serious I'll go half with you on buying this business, but you is going to have to pull your weight around here."

"Aight Dee, I'll do my part. Now let's go find this Arab bastard, kick his ass, take his bread, and use it to buy this business."

"Marilyn had remained quiet during the exchange between Black and I, and now she said "Dee, since you planning on doing the family thing you might want to consider buying one of my houses to move your family into."

Marilyn owned several houses through-out Brooklyn, Queens, and Long Island. The idea of moving Brittney and my son into our own house really appealed to me. I knew Brittney would love the idea, she was raised living in houses, not apartments, and I wanted to do right by her and our son. I wanted to be able to provide the best for both of them.

"Marilyn, when can you give me a tour of some of your houses? I need to check them out so I can see which one I'd like to buy."

"Dee, I'll give you the keys and addresses so you can go with

Enemies Amongst Us   D. Isaac

your old lady and check them out whenever you got time. Honestly though I think the one I'm living at in Long Island would be the best fit for you and your family."

"How much you want for the house your living at Marilyn?" I knew it had some fly shit if Marilyn was living in it. Baby girl had good taste.

"I want two hundred thousand for the property Dee, but don't trip I can help you get a mortgage."

"Alright girl, let me talk it over with my baby mama and I'll get back to you. I got to see how good her credit is."

"For sure Dee, you do that, but don't forget that I'm trying to get rid of everything and leave the country. So don't take to long to get back to me."

"A'ight ma, now give me Sayeed's address, so I can go check out his neighborhood.

"Hold on Dee, I'ma come with you and show you exactly where his bitch ass is living and what kind of car he is driving." she said, grabbing her bag and keys so she could lock up the store for the day.

Sayeed lived in a big apartment building across town in a neighborhood known as Sheepshed Bay. This neighborhood was populated with Russian Mafia members and Hasidic Jews. Not to many black people lived in this community. I knew immediately that we would have to be very discrete in order to run up on Sayeed and fuck with him around here. The Russian mafia didn't play and if they saw a couple of black guys beating on a white looking guy in this neighborhood they might chose to intervene.

Enemies Amongst Us   D. Isaac

On the same hand if the Jews saw us hanging around here to long they were likely to call the police on us because they knew we didn't belong around these parts. The Hasidic Jews, were just as powerful if not more powerful than the Russian mafia. They controlled the Diamond District and also Wall Street. They had a lot of business through-out the five boroughs. The Hasidic's had several communities through out the New York area and even their own security that patrolled their neighborhoods."

After we had been driving around Sayeed's neighborhoods for a few minutes I said to Marilyn "Sayeed chose wisely moving to this community. With his complexion he could blend in with either main faction here,"

"Yeah I got to give it to him." she replied, before adding "What do you think? it's going to be hard for you to get at him over here?"

"If there's a will there's a way baby girl. what time does he go to work?"

"He usually leaves the house about five in the morning." she replied.

"Where is his taxi at?" I asked, trying to gain any useful piece of knowledge I could.

"He doesn't keep it over here. It's in a garage in Queens. That's his car right over there." she said, as she pointed out a blue Toyota Camry.

"What do you think Black?" I asked, thinking he might have some useful input or something significant that might have escaped my eye.

Enemies Amongst Us   D. Isaac

"It could be done, we just got to be laying on him when he comes out of his building, and get him back in it before he gets to his car."

"Alright Marilyn, I got this, we've seen enough." I said, as I drove off to take her back to her car. I already knew what I needed to do in order to get him. Black's plan was the exact same as mine, all we had to do was park in front of his building in one of our cars with dark window tints and wait for him to come out. Soon as he made his exit, we'd rush him, take him back inside the building, tie him up, find his look, and kick his teeth in for good measure.

By the time I had dropped Marilyn off at her car it was getting late in the evening so I decided to call it a night.

"Yo, son I'ma call it a night." I told Black

"What we gone do with them cards tomorrow ?" he asked

"I'ma grab Stephanie and Dave in the morning and we could go over New jersey and burn up Circuit City and Best Electronic stores and all the mail and outlets we see over there."

"Cool, that sounds like a plan. I"ll see you in morning then." Black said, exiting my car when I pulled up in front of his crib."

After I dropped Black off I was feeling hungry, so I went and grab two orders of some akee and salt fish with some dumplings and boiled bananas and yams with some carrot juice from Sally's Jamaican restaurant on Rutland Ave. to take home for me and Brittney.

The following morning after I picked up Black, I went and got my home girl Stephanie then Dave. Dave was this homosexual

Enemies Amongst Us　　　　　　　　　　D. Isaac

dude that had moved to New York from Alabama . Dave was about 6'2" and 260 pounds. The brother was built like a football player, but he was gay as a mutha fucka. He had moved to New York to make a better life for himself, but when things didn't' work-out as he had planned. He asked Stephanie to hook him up with something to do so he could make some money and she had introduced him to me. So now I had Dave on my payroll shopping with cards for me.

We hit New Jersey on a shopping frenzy, by evening time we had my Dodge Caravan damn near filled with laptop computers, and all types of clothing.

On our way back home, just before we left New Jersey we saw one last Mall and Black said "Yo son, I still got one more card with $500 on it. Lets stop here so I can get another computer."

"Yo, why don't you just hold on to that card until tomorrow and use it in the city at Radio Shack?" I asked.

"Nah Dee, I want to get this shit over with now." He replied.

I was tired and ready to get the hell out of New Jersey, but I still went against my better judgment and pulled into the mall so Black could spend the money that was on the card.

After about 30 minutes while me and Black was sitting in the van waiting on Stephanie and Dave to come back out of the mall I noticed a white van that kept circling the parking lot in the mall.

"Yo son, you peep that white van over there? I asked him. "Yeah son, I been peeped it, something must be up, plus they taking to long." He replied.

Enemies Amongst Us										D. Isaac

A few minutes later I said, "Aigh't here comes Stephanie out the door now but where is Dave?"

When Stephanie got into the car she said, " I think something is wrong, they taking to long with Dave, like they stalling for something."

After she said that, I moved the van to another spot where we could still see the exit if Dave came out of the mall. This way I could see if he was being followed and wouldn't lead the police right to us.

About 5 minutes later Dave came out of the mall empty handed and I noticed the white van started moving like it was stalking him from a distance. He was walking to the spot where he thought the van was still parked, I hurriedly drove over to him and he jumped in real quick and I drove out of the mall.

As I pulled out of the mall parking lot the white van drove up behind me and started flashing its lights like a cop car.

"Yo, can you believe this shit? The fucking rent-a-cop is trying to pull me over." I said.

"Man fuck him, keep going. Besides that they ain't got any authority outside the mall parking lot anyway." Black said.

I wasn't planning on stopping anyway, and as we drove further away from the mall the van kept on pursuing us, so I floored it heading for the Outer-Bridge Crossing which lead to Staten Island and out of the state of New Jersey.

Just before we got to the ramp to go over the bridge we see a New Jersey police car blocking the entrance way while the white

Enemies Amongst Us   D. Isaac

van was still behind us.

""Yo son, I'm still on parole, if I get caught over here that's a violation, and I ain't trying to go back to jail." Black said.

"Hey, I got a warrant out for me in Alabama, and I don't want to get caught neither." Dave bursts out panicking all of a sudden.

"A'ight this is what I'ma do. I'm going to pull over to the side by the guard railing on my right over there and when I do ya'll jump out and dive over the rail right there and make a run for it. Get the fuck out of here." then turning to Stephanie. "You stay with me."

"Alright Dee. lets do it." They all agreed.

When I started to pull over to the side, the cop car in front of me moves over to stay in front of me and open up the entrance way to the bridge. I just acted like we was going to surrender, but instead I put the van in neutral, Black and Dave both jumped out and flew over the rail.

As soon as they were out of sight, I dropped the gear back down into drive and went around the cop car, flooring it over the bridge, not slowing down until I made it to the Verrazano Bridge taking me back to Brooklyn.

Stephanie was quiet the whole time, all of a sudden as soon as we got over the Verrazano she said, "Dee, pull over at the next exit I got to pee."

"Damn girl, you can't wait until I get you home?"

"Nah, nigga I got to pee now damn it. Shit you had me sweating

Enemies Amongst Us   D. Isaac

bullets for the last 15 minutes. I thought our ass was sure going to jail. You are one crazy driving mutha fucka Dee. Now hurry up and pull over right there before I pee on myself."

My home girl Stephanie was a real down ass good chick. Later on when shit hit the fan with me and my crew she would keep it real and give the feds false information about me. She never flipped under pressure always keeping it "G"

After I dropped Steph at her crib, I took my ass home. While laying in my bed about 1AM, I get a call from Black stating he was outside my house. When I went outside to talk to him he told me how he and Dave had separated when they went over the rail and how he had broke into somebody's basement and hid until he felt it was safe to come out. He then went, and found a store in the neighborhood and called a cab to get him out of there. When I asked him why he had to come to my spot this late, he said he wanted his share of the stuff we bought earlier.

As I thought about it later on as time went by, and I found out how the Feds work. Either Black had so much larceny in his heart and he didn't trust me to keep his stuff until the morning or he had gotten caught that night in New Jersey and he had made arrangements to have him release right away and he led them to my house,so they could put me under surveillance. The game done changed. There is no such thing as death before dishonor anymore. I even here these young guys with a saying now about.

"Why do Ten when you can tell on a friend"

Chapter 29

One morning at about 11 AM, I was by myself at my stash house counting some money to pay Marilyn for her real-estate business and planning my day, I got a call on me cell from a blocked number.

"Talk to me." I said, answering it never being one to dodge a call even if it was from a blocked number.

"What's up Dee? How are you doing?" Lola, Denise's friend, asked through the other end.

"I'm fine Lola, what's up with you?"

"Dee I need to talk to you, can you come pick me up from in front of my school at about 1 this afternoon?"

"Is everything good with you girl? You iight?" Lola had never called me on her own before.

"Yeah Dee, I'm good, I just need to talk to you about something. That's all. So can you pick me up or not? And Dee please come by yourself."

"Sure Ma, I'll be there." I said, my curiosity peaked.

Lola's school, also known as BMCC, was located on the lower west side of Manhattan, a few blocks over form the World Trade Center. As I sat in my truck admiring all the beautiful college girls and working women on their lunch breaks, I felt blessed to be alive and living in America. I looked over to my right and saw the twin towers standing there, I also thought about Marilyn's husband

Enemies Amongst Us

D. Isaac

Sayeed and his trying to blow up those magnificent buildings and kill everybody inside of them, and the thought angered me to say the least.

I was so deep in my thoughts that I didn't see Lola when she approached my vehicle. "Damn Dee, what you thinking so hard about?" she said, breaking my trance.

"Just thinking about some business I got to handle for a friend, that's all." I said reassuring her, as she climbed into the passenger side of my truck and I drove off.

So how was your day? How are you doing? I asked, still curious about what she wanted to talk to me about.

"Dee, I know you and Denise is fucking, she told me that you wasn't her man, and the two of you are just friends with no strings attached. Also she told me how you be looking out for her and helping her out with her bill and stuff." she said, looking me in the eyes.

"And?" I responded, wondering where she was going with this.

"Well she told me how she be sucking your dick and how ya'll be getting y'all freak on. So I was wondering if I could get down with you like that too."

"What exactly do you mean by get down like that too?" I asked, surprised that this was what she wanted to talk to me about.

"Dee, I want some of that dick to, I can suck and fuck better than Denise ever dreamed of, and I could use a little help with my bills as well."

Enemies Amongst Us

D. Isaac

"Lola, is you trying me? Did Denise put you up to this?" I asked, thinking she was up to something.

"Hell no Dee, ain't nobody trying to set you up. I ain't got any time for them type of childish games. I got bills to pay besides I told her that I wanted your number to talk to you about some checks. So we is gonna keep this between us, right?"

"Word, sounds like a plan. You really think you can suck dick better than Denise huh?"

"Hell yeah that bitch ain't got shit on me."

"Show me what you got then, let me be the judge of your skills." I told her, setting the test to see if she was really serious.

"When, right now?" she asked.

"No tomorrow, at 3:61 of course right now." we was in traffic and it was the middle of the day with all kinds of people walking by the truck. Luckily I had tint on the windows, so they couldn't see into it clearly.

"Papi you ain't said a word." Lola said, reaching over the console, unzipping my pants, putting my dick in her mouth and going to work deep throating it and licking the sides up and down like a pro.

Lola was just as good as Denise or a little bit better. She was very pretty, she had a flawless body, and didn't have any kids. The only thing was she still lived with her mother, so there would be no going up in her spot late at night. I had to keep my episodes with her during the day time when Denise and Brittney were at work. It was all good. A true playa knows how to juggle his women and

Enemies Amongst Us   D. Isaac

spend enough time with each to keep them happy.

As time progressed, I started spending a lot of time with Lola and she had gotten real comfortable with me. While we were riding around in the city after I had picked her up form school one afternoon she looked at me and asked,

"Hey Dee, how come you don't eat my pussy?"

"I calmly looked at her and responded "Gangsta's don't eat pussy baby girl. Where I come from that shit is taboo. Did Denise tell you I eat her pussy?

No, she says you don't be eating her out."

"So ya'll be talking about me then, huh?"

"No, she be talking. I just be listening to her when she tells me stuff. That's how I knew that you like getting your dick sucked. She told me how the two of you met and how you took her to a fancy restaurant in little Italy.

"What else she been telling you?

"Nothing bad just how good you be fucking her and looking out for her, stuff like that. You know girl talk basically."

"That's all ya'll be talking about?"

"Yeah that's about it, Dee do you know any girls that be eating pussy? I ain't ever had a girl go down on me before and I wanted to try it." She said, looking at me gauging my reaction.

"Yeah I know some." replied smoothly.

Enemies Amongst Us	D. Isaac

"can you hook me up Papi? Can you take me to one of them bitches and have them suck my pussy?"

"I got you mami. Don't trip, I'ma hook you up." I said, busting an illegal U-turn and heading back to my stash crib in Clinton Hills.

My friend Renee that lived in my building was bi-sexual and she always had some girls hanging out at her crib. I called her on my cell and asked her if Stephanie was there and she told me yes. that was all the clearance I needed. The playa in me was ready to watch some girl on girl action.

Stephanie was another girl that I gave cards to and shopped with me. She was a cute, chubby, short brown skinned chick, barely pushing 5' tall in heels. Stephanie was, what one would call a real around-the-way girl. She had a good personality and was always fun to be around. Also she was bi-sexual and had confied in me, when we were out shopping, that she liked eating pussy and needed a girl real bad cause she hadn't had one for a while. Putting two and two together I knew Lola would be a treat for her, but as usual I made sure I'd benefit from the situation also.

When we got to my stash house, I left Lola in my apartment and went upstairs to Renee's to tell Stephanie what I wanted her to do. She knew I had good taste in females and agreed to come downstairs with me and handle this business after talking me into buying her a pair of shoes the next time we went shopping.

After I introduces Stephanie to Lola, I told her to take off her clothes and get in the bed. When Steph saw Lola's body, she started salivating at the mouth.

Enemies Amongst Us   D. Isaac

Lola had one of those perfect bodies, the type you see on the cover of Straight Stuntin magazines. Her breasts stood up with out the support of a bra, her stomach was flat and smooth, and most importantly her pussy was cleanly shaved. She just looked so smooth and soft like a woman is supposed to be. I knew Stephanie wasn't going to take her clothes off after seeing Lola's body. All she could do was just go to work on her.

"'Your sexy Lola." Steph told her.

"Thank you, your very pretty yourself." Lola replied.

"I love your breasts."

"Do you want to feel them?"

As Stephanie squeezed her breasts Lola bit her lip, looked over at me, and smiled.

Steph then started sucking on her tits, and flicking her tongue on the nipples.

Taking her time, giving her the ultimate foreplay, Stephanie took Lola down a slow erotic journey, working her tongue down to Lola's wetness eventually parting her pussy lips.

When Lola let out a moan of pure ecstasy, and started rambling in Spanish. I pulled my chair closer to the bed so I could get a better view of the action.

Lola's eyes were rolled up in her head, and she had a fistful of Stephanie's hair pulling it like she was trying to rip it right out of her scalp.

Stephanie was sucking on Lola 's clit and tonguing her pussy driving her wild.

"Aye mija, aye mija, I'm cumming." Lola burst out switching back and forth from Spanish to English in a confusing blur of words.

As I watched the pleasure that Lola was getting from what Stephanie was doing to her I felt jealous that I had never pleased a woman like that before. I said to myself that I have to learn to do that shit. I was going to have to get some pussy eating lesson form Steph, I just couldn't let any of my boys know about that cause they'd clown the fuck out of me.

Sucking pussy is taboo in some cultures, and I didn't grow up with people who did it. I was never taught to do that. One of my friends who is a captain in the Italian Mafia, later told me that if a guy was a cunt sucker he could not become a member of their organization, and if they were to find out that a member was doing it, he could be killed or made to pay a fine depending on his status with them. They felt that if a guy could put a woman's vagina in his mouth, he could do anything, including telling on his friends. Cunt suckers didn't have any scruples.

Enemies Amongst Us   D. Isaac

Chapter 30

I had not gotten a chance to see Pierre when I was down in Atlantic City with my boys. So I needed to go back down there to see him, so I could collect my share of the profits from the counterfeits he and Rick had switched out for me.

I also had not been spending much time with Denise, and Brittney was getting on my nerves more and more nagging the shit out of me. I needed to get away from her and relax for a little bit, especially after the close call with the pigs in Jersey. I decided to pick up Denise and take her down to Americas playground with me.

Denise was really happy to get away with me for the weekend. When we got to Atlantic City, Pierre had a room reserved for me on the 18th floor of Bally's. after I had collected my $14,000 from him, I took her shopping and bought her a pair of Gucci shoes along with a matching pocket-book and sunglasses.

After dinner and a few drinks later on that night we went back upstairs to get our freak on before I hit the black Jack tables.

Once we were back in the room we decided to take a shower together, Denise washed me from head to toe like I was her African king, While she was washing my back she started licking her way down, She stooped down behind me and started washing my ass, and the next thing I knew, she was licking my ass and sucking my balls from behind. All of the sudden my body started tingling and my toes curled up. The sensation of her tongue going in circles on my asshole along with her blowing warm air on me had my dick

Enemies Amongst Us — D. Isaac

hard as the rock that makes up Mt. Rushmore.

Then she turned me around and took me in her mouth and started deep throating me, licking up and down the sides of my dick. When I came she swallowed every drop, and told me how much she appreciated the quality time we were spending together.

After the shower we made love on the bed, when we got tired of the bed I took her to the window and had her kneel down on the chair, facing the ocean like I had done with the girl me and Carlos tag teamed.

I realized that I liked the view of the Atlantic Ocean, especially when I had to look over Denise's soft round ass as I was hitting it from the back.

I was so turned on I felt like superman. The thrill of only a piece of glass keeping us form falling to our deaths while making love excited me and Denise even more.

Her pussy was soaking wet from all the fucking we were doing. When I slipped out of her on the back stroke she moaned.

"Dee, put it in my ass."

I couldn't believe my ear, so I asked "What?" like a damn fool.

"Fuck me in the ass Dee." she said, again reaching between her legs to grab my dick and guide it to the entrance of her asshole.

Denise then hooked her ankles around my legs to keep me hooked to her and started gyrating that ass at me. Talk about face down ass up. I didn't need any more encouragement.

i didn't want to hurt her, so I licked my fingers, and gently

Enemies Amongst Us — D. Isaac

inserted one into her ass to loosen her up. When she started bucking back on my finger, I slammed another one in there.

That got a soft moan out of her and she said, "Damn Dee. that feels so good."

I knew she was ready now, so I took my fingers out and entered her, and started stroking her gently letting her get used to me.

"That's right Dee, fuck my ass, fuck me baby." she begged.

When I heard her say that, I grabbed her by the waist and pulled her into me going deep as possible. I was so turned on I started pulling her hair as she arched her back, I bit her on her neck and started sucking on her like I was count Dracula.

I had never had a woman initiate anal sex with me before. I wasn't getting none of this treatment at home, and I knew if Denise kept this shit up she was going to be in my life for a very long time. She was taking me to new sexual heights and I was loving every minute of it. I didn't know if she was on the E pill "Ecstasy" or not but she was sure freaking me like she was. I was starting to wonder if she had slipped me one cause I was sure feeling extra freaky myself.

Denise and I fucked all over our hotel room that night and after we had finished fucking I had to take another shower before getting dressed and going downstairs to get my gamble on. Denise didn't gamble and it was already late so she just wanted to stay in bed and get some sleep.

It was about 2 AM and I was back at the Black Jack tables when I looked up and saw Brittney and her friend Sharon about 10 isles over form me walking up and down looking for me.

Enemies Amongst Us   D. Isaac

I quickly grabbed my chips off the table, ducked down and backed away until I was behind some slot machines. I then backed out of the casino floor unseen by Brittney and Sharon and headed straight for the elevators.

When I got upstairs to my room I woke up Denise and explained "Baby I need you to get up, get dressed and take a cab back to New York."

"What's wrong baby?" she asked.

"My wifey is downstairs with her girlfriend looking for me." I told her keeping it real. This is why you always stay upfront with your side chick.

"Oh shit." she responded.

"Listen here is $500, go down to the front of the casino and get a taxi to take you back home, and I will see you when I get back."

"Alright Baby," Denise said, getting up and getting dressed in a hurry. before helping me clean up the room and making a quick exit.

That was another reason Denise was a keeper, She didn't argue or fuss, she knew her position and played it to the T. After I had gave her the money and she was on her way out the door she said, "Baby I'ma take the damn bus and save some of this money. I ain't wasting all this money on no damn cab. Shit I ain't in no rush to get home now ", and she was gone.

Before I left the room I made sure everything was spotless and I turned up the air-conditioner on high so the room would air out.

Enemies Amongst Us

D. Isaac

When I got back on the casino floor, I went and sat back down at the Black Jack tables and started gambling while waiting for Brittney to come find me.

When her and Sharon walked up on me, I acted surprised to see them and said, " Hi baby, what ya'll doing down here?"

Now that she had found me she just looked around and asked, "Why haven't you been answering your phone?"

"You know cell phones don't work inside the casino baby. What's this, you came down here to fight with me?" I asked, hopping to the offensive.

I have been calling your phone and beeping you all day, and you haven't been answering or calling me back", she fusses.

"Look I needed to get away, so I came down here so I can relax, and get away from all the bullshit, that's all. How did you know to find me here anyway?" I asked, trying to keep my cool.

"When I couldn't get you, I decided to call down here and ask if you was registered at the casino and they told me yes, so I drove down to come and meet you."

"You came down here to chill with me or spy on me?" Brittney and her friend were wearing jeans and timberland boots, both had their hair tied up in pony tails. They was dressed for a rumble, they didn't normally dress like this, they were working and classy girls. So I knew what they were up to, but I was not going to make it easy for her.

"Let me get the key to your room." she asked, throwing me a suspicious glare, resting one hand on her cocked hip, and sticking

Enemies Amongst Us							D. Isaac

the other palm up like she finally got me figured out.

"What for?" I asked, just to push her buttons.

"Sharon needs to use the restroom."

'There's a bathroom right out the door right there." I said, pointing in the direction of where it was.

"She won't use that one, she says it's dirty."

"Girl stop playing, you know they got somebody in there cleaning the bathroom 24/7."

"Just give me the key to your room Dee." she snapped then added "She wants to use that one and I'ma a little tired after the drive down here", not giving an inch. Her eyes and body language letting me know she wasn't going to quit till she had that key. A look of triumph like she had finally caught me slipping, thinking when we went up to my room she was going to find a girl up there.

"Alright baby. I hope you find what your looking for." I conceded, handing her the keys to my room, and laughing to myself.

About 20 minutes later they came back downstairs looking disappointed. I watched Brittney go and sit down at a closed Black Jack table, as Sharon approached me.

"Dee, she sorry." Sharon said, rubbing me on my back.

"Sharon's she is driving me crazy with all of this jealous and insecure shit." I told her playing the good, angry husband role.

"I know Dee, but just forgive her and be patient with her. She

Enemies Amongst Us — D. Isaac

loves you very much."

"I love her to Sharon, but she got to learn how to trust me, when we're not around each other. You don't see me spying on her, do you?"

"I know you love her Dee, just don't be mad at her. I'm going to go and talk to her." she said, going back over to Brittney.

It was about 4 AM and I didn't feel like gambling anymore, so I told Brittney and Sharon that we should go get some sleep and we'd leave in the morning.

Brittney was happy that I was not mad at her for coming down here to spy on me, and willing to do anything I told her to do, in order to make it up to me.

A true playa got to know how to think on his feet and be able to flip the script on his woman, also he had to be able to adapt when his back was against the wall, if he was going to survive in this game. A real playa had also got to be able to keep his mistress happy and keep it real with them. Had I not been upfront, who knows what kind of shit storm I would've had to deal with out of Denise when I told her my wife was downstairs. I was taught this by one of the best old school pimps in Brooklyn had back in the days, Pimpin Joe. I was so smooth, I had Brittney telling me how sorry she was. All's well, that ends well.

Talk about a close call, I knew from now on I had to be more careful. In the future every time I was gonna take a vacation to the lovely Atlantic City with a shortie, I would defiantly be registering in a different name, just in case Brittney started any of her CIA bullshit.

Chapter 31

A couple days after my close call with Brittney in Atlantic City, I was back on my grind. I was driving around in my Dodge Caravan with Denise and Lola both, and we had been out shopping at Macy's department store on 34th in Manhattan. When I got a call on my cell form a number I didn't recognize, even though it carried a 212 area code.

"What's up Dread? How're you doing?" it was Curtis, my counterfeit connection that had been lining my pocket with all the sweet paper I've been living on lately.

Alarms started going off in my head for some reason. Curtis never called me from a 212 number. 212 was Manhattan business, or residents. Curtis had a 718 number cause he lived in the Bronx, so I found this new number a little strange.

"Ain't nothing Curtis". I replied, before asking "What's up with you?"

"Same shit Dread, I got some more of that fake money for you. How much you want to buy?" He asked putting both our business on the phone like he specifically refused to do the first time, and every other time we talked about it.

"What the fuck are you talking about Curtis?" I asked, then added " I don't know anything about any fucking money." for good measure before hanging up on him.

He must not have known I had caller ID on my cell phone, because after I hung up, I waited a few minutes then called the

Enemies Amongst Us   D. Isaac

number back. It rang a couple times before a chippy professional voice answered.

"United States Secret Service. How may I direct your call?"

I almost broke my phone pressing the button so hard to disconnect the call. I knew I smelled a rat, and it was this mutha fucka Curtis, trying to set me up with the Secret Service.

After I'd hung up the phone my whole vibe changed. I didn't want to shop anymore, and I definitely couldn't concentrate on shit. I felt like eyes were watching me everywhere.

"What's wrong baby?" Denise asked, picking up my vibe "Did you get some bad news?"

"Yeah one of my boys just called me form the secret service office, the nigga is trying to set me up yo!" I exclaimed, before continuing " I'ma take y'all home, I need to fall back and figure this shit out." I finished, and we started heading over to the West Side Highway to take them back uptown to where they all lived.

The next day as I was leaving my house, I got another call on my cell form yet another 212 number, and when I answered it, I heard an unfamiliar voice on the other end.

"Hello Dexter, my name is agent Jack Bower and I'm with the Secret Service."

All kinds of thoughts started racing through my head, should I hang up, throw the phone out of the window, are they behind me right now? I had never gotten a call from the Secret Service, all I knew was those were the guys that guarded the president. I couldn't for the life of me figure out what they wanted with me.

I decided to see what he wanted, so I asked sarcastically "Hello, and what can I do for you secret agent man?"

"Dexter I would like you to come down to the secret Service office in Manhattan, so we can talk. If you come down here you have my word that I'm not going to arrest you."

"When do you want me to come there?" I asked, my curiosity getting the better of me.

"Well today is Thursday and the president is coming in tomorrow, so Monday morning would be the best for me. Write my number down and make sure to give me a call when your on your way."

"Okay." I agreed, as I he recited his number and I took it down before ending the call.

I was so fucked up in my head by that call, I had to pull over to the side of the road before I had an accident. I kept asking myself if I had ever done anything to Bill Clinton, so why the fuck would the Secret Service want to talk to me. I was naive to the law at the time and didn't know that the Secret Service was part of the Treasury Department, and therefore handled all counterfeit investigations.

I decided to call Melvin Krinsky, an attorney I kept on retainer. Melvin and his brother operated a law office located at 50 Court St. in downtown Brooklyn. Melvin had represented me a few times in court and had always managed to get my cases thrown out.

"Good afternoon Melvin, this is Dexter Isaac. How are you doing?" I greeted him, after his secretary had patched me through."

Enemies Amongst Us
D. Isaac

"Hey Dex, I'm fine how are you?" He asked, then added " You ain't locked up again, are you?" with a tone of laughter in his voice.

"Nah Melvin, I'm not locked up, but I do need your help with something." Melvin had an easy manor always joking with his clients to put them at ease even though most were facing prison time.

"Okay Dex, what seems to be the problem?"

"I got a call form this guy claiming to be the Secret Service, he said he wants me to come down to their office Monday so we can talk, and he promises that he is not going to arrest me. I may need you to roll down there with me. What's your schedule look like Monday Melvin?"

"Don't tell me you tried to sell some of that weed you got to the President." He replied, laughing at his own joke.

"Fuck no Melvin, I didn't try to sell that base head no weed." I responded, laughing along with him despite being nervous about my new found situation.

"Dex give me this guys number, so I can call him and find out what's this all about, then I'll call you back." He said, then took down the number before disconnecting the call and going about his business.

No more than 30 minutes later, he called me back and the first words out of his mouth were " Dex, I don't want you going down there to meet those guys." His concern obvious.

"What happened Melvin? What did you find out?" I asked, worrying more every minute.

Resorting to his usual humor he joked " they want to make a clone of you for the President." then cracked up laughing.

"What the fuck are you talking about Melvin." I snapped, getting fed up with his jokes. Here I am nervous as hell and this fuck wants to be Jim fucking Carey.

"I don't want you going down there because I know how you feel about rats and they want to turn you into one. That's why they want you to come down to their office. I told that guy not to call you again, and if he has anything to say to you or ask you about he should contact me first, being I am the attorney that represents you."

'Thanks Melvin, you the man." I said, gratefully.

"Your welcome Dex, however I do need to see you at my office by 6 PM, with $500 in hand." He said and ended the call. I couldn't help but think at that point that every bad attorney joke I'd ever heard was true.

I felt a lot better after my call with Melvin knowing that he was on top of things. However once again I was being naive, I thought I was doing the right thing by calling my attorney, and exercising my rights. What I didn't know was that I had just made an enemy of Agent Jack Bower and he was going to carry a vendetta against me. He didn't stop until he had me locked up and he used any means necessary.

Chapter 32

As time went by and I didn't hear anything else from agent Bower, I let me guard down and got comfortable, once again falling back into my old routine. Black and I went half and gave Marilyn the $10,000 for her real estate business. Then we hired my neighbor Renee to work as our secretary in the office.

Everything was going smooth, then Black started acting suspect all of the sudden. Ever since that episode in New Jersey he had been acting kind of funny. He wasn't coming around as much anymore, and every time I called him to go do something with me, he would say he couldn't leave his house for long, or he couldn't go far from his house cause his parole officer was sweating him. He kept coming up with all kinds of excuses not to hangout, so we could start the recon on sayeed mark ass. He gave me his word he'd help me kick Sayeed's ass, and before he would've been chomping at the bit for the chance to rob his bitch ass. Now he was flaking on me, so I decided to call Mugsy up and take him with with me to rob Sayeed instead.

"What's up rude boy? What have you been up?" I asked him, when he answered his phone.

"Man Dex, shit is all fucked up, starr." He responded, sounding all stressed the fuck out.

"What's wrong my youth?" I asked.

"Starr, I went on a jux with Panama and Penicole from Flatbush. The jux was up in the Bronx and when we picked the locks and went into the house the people were home and we got into a shoot out with them. By the time we made it back outside the house and into our car the cops were coming and they chased us. We had to throw our guns away before we shook them and got away."

"Did you get hurt?"

"Nah, I'm good. Ain't none of us got hurt, but we lit their asses up in that house before we got the hell out of there though." Mugs bragged, laughing like the whole thing was dangerous but amusing at the same time to him.

"That's good to hear that your alright rude-boy."

'So what's up with you Dex?"

"I got a jux I was thinking about taking you on with me."

"Word?"

"Yeah, this Arab mutha fucka is trying to play one of my home girls. She gave me his info and I told her that I was going to fuck him up for her and rob his bitch ass."

"How much we looking at?"

"She said he keeps about 50 grand in his house, cause he don't like keeping his money in the banks."

"Starr I'm down to go with you, but you is going to have to get me a tool. Remember I told you we had to throw ours away when the cops were chasing us."

"I got you, I'ma get one for you right now, let me call you back." I told him, before ending the call.

Enemies Amongst Us   D. Isaac

Carlos was out of town, so I called Black, cause I knew he kept a few guns around from all the burglaries he'd been doing."

"Yo son, I need to come by your crib and talk to you for a minute." I said, as soon as he answered the phone.

"I'm at my cousins house on church Ave. and 94th St."

"Blacks cousin lived in east Flatbush and I was in Carnasie, so I said "Yo, i'ma be there in 15 minutes."

"Alright I'll see you when you get here." He said, as I ended the call.

When I pulled up in front of Blacks cousins house he was sitting outside on the steps waiting for me. He hopped up, came over and got in the car with me.

"What's up Dee? What you need to talk about?" He asked, getting straight to the point.

"Yo son, I need to borrow a burner from you for Mugs. He lost his the other day and I'm gong to take him with me to handle that thing with Marilyn's husband." I explained.

"I got a .38 Smith and Wesson pistol he can use, But I want it back soon as he buys another one.

"Okay, that'll have to work." i told him.

Aight, hold on a minute, I got to go inside the house, just wait right here while I go and get it." He said, getting out of the car.

After I had gotten the pistol from Black I called Mugsy back. "Rude-boy I got that tool for you from Black, but he said to tell you he wants it back as soon as you buy another one." I told him.

"Yeah man Dex, No problem, I got you starr." He said, in his unmistakable Jamaican drawl.

"What you doing right now, you want me to bring it by your crib?" I asked.

"Yeah, bring it over. I'll see you when you get here." He said ending the call.

When I arrived at Mugsy's house in Queens about 45 minutes later, I find him chilling with his kids. He had 2 daughters and 3 boys. The 3 youngest ones ranged form ages 4-7 and they were driving him crazy. His wife Sheryl had gotten a job as a secretary in a real estate office so he was stuck in the house until she got home everyday. When I gave him the gun he went and stashed it in the basement of his house, while I stayed upstairs and played with the kids. I gave the 4 younger ones $20. each and his eldest daughter $50. they loved uncle Dex. I knew things were tough for Mugs and his family and he was trying to do the best he could, being a product of the ghetto.

Mugsy was a high school drop-out without any vocational skills and no type of job training. Like most young men growing up in the streets all he knew about was survival; selling drugs, and robbing people whatever it took in order to get the money to feed his family.

Like many other ghetto youths, I had also gotten my PHD "Playa/hustling Degree" from the streets. The streets had taught me chemistry, sociology, and philosophy.

After I had spent about an hour with Mugs and his clan, I got a

Enemies Amongst Us

D. Isaac

call from Brenda.

"What's up Dex, what're you doing?" she asked, when I answered the phone.

"Nothing just chillin out with my boy Mugs and his kids at their spot in Queens." I explained.

"You got any money on you?" she asked, even though she already knew the answer was yes.

"Yeah, I got some, why? what's up?" I responded.

"I need $200."

"Oh yeah? What you going to do for me if I give it to you?" I asked her. Testing her to see what she would say.

"Whatever you want me to do."

Brenda had some good ass head, and I hadn't got any from her since we had broken up, honesty I missed it and I was getting kind of horny just thinking about it and hearing her voice on the phone "I want some head."

"Alright where do you want to meet at?" she responded.

"Meet me in the Green Acres Mall parking lot on the Sunrise highway in front of Wal-Mart."

"I'll be there in 20 minutes." she said, hanging up the phone.

"Yo, Mugs I gotta run, I'll catch you tomorrow and we can go look at that job I told you about. I told him, heading out the door.

"Alright rude boy. Make sure you put some rubbers on your

Willie and don't be silly." He joked. laughing as he quoted the Jamaican Reggae superstar Buju Banton.

I met up with Brenda in the McDonalds parking lot and she gave me the best blow job in her life. She sucked me like she was auditioning for one of those Black Video Illustrated Videos.

We would go on to make this a regular thing. We developed a routine, every week she would call me asking for money, and I would respond that I need a blowjob, Then we would meet somewhere and do the damn thing. Either in her car or mine

I couldn't figure Brenda out, I knew her family had money and she really didn't need any from me. I came to the conclusion one day that she was just missing me and now she had an excuse to spend some time with me or she just wanted to get back at Brittney for ruining our marriage.

Chapter 33

Christmas was quickly approaching, and I need to make as much extra money as I possibly could. I was quickly learning that having a family and couple of women in my life were very expensive.

I had to get my priorities in order, I had to teach Sayeed a lesson for messing with my friend Marilyn and all the innocent people that had gotten hurt or killed at the World Trade Center.

I also had to have a talk with Brittney about buying Marilyn's house, so I decided to talk to her about it one evening when she came home from work.

"Baby my friend Marilyn is moving back to France to be with her daughter and she wants to sell me her house in Long Island before she leaves." I told her.

"That sounds great baby, are you going to buy it?" she asked.

"Yeah, I want tot buy it, but I got to put it in your name because I haven't been working. I don't want the IRS to come and take it from us after we get it."

"Baby you can put it in my name. You know I pay my taxes, but I don't know if my credit is good enough for us to get a mortgage."

I know this mortgage broker downtown, we can go by his office tomorrow on your lunch beak and see if he can get you a mortgage."

"Okay baby, that sounds good." She said.

The next day we went to see the mortgage broker. After he ran a credit check on Brittney he told us that her credit was to low to get the $180,000 mortgage we needed to buy the house.

"Brittney was looking very disappointed by the news, but I was not ready to give up. I decided to call Marilyn and see if she had any connections with mortgage brokers.

"Bonjour Mademoiselle." (hello Madame) I greeted her in French when she answered her phone.

'Bonjour Dee." she responded.

"Commet allez-vous?" (How are you) I asked her.

"Bien merci" (fine thank you)

"Marilyn I'm having problems getting somebody to give Brittney a mortgage." I told her, after we'd finished the pleasantries.

"Dee, I'm going to come by the real estate office tomorrow, and we will work it out. Don't worry about that, I know how we can get around it", she said reassuringly.

"Alright girl, thank you, I'll see tomorrow afternoon when you roll through." I agreed, as we ended the call.

The following day I was in the office with Mugs talking with Marilyn when Black decided to show up.

"Dee, in order to make this transaction go through, I think we should do a deed transfer instead of a direct sale. This is what I'm gong to do for you because I want to leave the country right away. I bought the house for $202,000 and I put another $30,00 into

Enemies Amongst Us   D. Isaac

fixing it up. So the house has $30,00 in equity in it. Just give me the $20,000 I put down to buy the house and I will transfer the deed to your wife's name and all you will have to do is take over the mortgage payment.

When the market gets better you can sell the house from anywhere between $240,000-$250,000, and pay the bank off keeping all the equity for yourself."

"Damn baby girl, that sounds like a plan. Lets do that then." I told her, amazed at the deal she was about to give me.

Black and Mugsy were quiet the entire time while Marilyn and I had been talking, but after hearing the deal she was giving me they both asked "Marilyn, you got any more houses your trying to sell like that?"

"I got a couple more houses for sale, but ya'll are going to have to go through the real estate broker that's handling the sale for me. I'm only doing this for Dee cause we have been friends for some time now.

I thought I saw a flicker of envy and jealousy come across both Black's and Mug's faces as Marilyn responded to their question. However instead of filing it away and taking heed of their expression, I dismissed it because of my happiness had me caught up in the moment.

"Dee, I'ma call you in a couple of days so you and your lady can come meet me at my attorneys office, so we can get the paper work signed and transferred." She said, as she grabbed her bag and headed for the door.

After Marilyn had left, Black said "Damn son, she must really like you. She is looking out for you. I wish I had a friend like that."

"Yeah rude boy, that's a good deal she giving you. Shit I wish somebody would give me a house with $30,00 in equity in it." Mugsy added.

"you must be fucking her huh Dex?" Black asked.

"Watch your mouth son, have some fucking respect. you both know she is just my friend." I told them, starting to get me upset.

"My bad Dex, I didn't mean anything by it." Black quickly back tracked.

"Don't worry about it, anyway I'm out of here. Mugs lets bounce." I said, heading for the door.

After me and Mugs left the office, I drove over to where Sayeed was living so I could show him the neighborhood.

"Yo, you see that big building on the right over there?" I asked him.

'"Yeah."

"He lives in there on the 3rd floor. We got to get him early in the morning about 5 o'clock when he comes out to go to work. When he makes his exit, all we got to do is back him down and take him back upstairs to his apartment, then tie his ass up , find the money and fuck his ass up before we leave."

"Why you want to fuck him up rude boy?" Mugs asked knowing it wasn't my normal routine to cause more damage than necessary.

"Because his bitch ass is trying to play my friend Marilyn and

Enemies Amongst Us					D. Isaac

he is one of the dudes that had something to do with that bomb going off in the garage at the World Trade Center." I explained.

"Word? He on that Al-Queda shit?"

"Yeah, Marilyn told me that one of the dudes that was in the van that day was his cousin. Also how her husband and some of his friends had cooked a lamb at her house the night before they detonated the bomb celebrating and talking about how they were going to sink fear into the American infidel dogs."

"Damn rude boy, I know some people that worked in them buildings over there. We gwan fuck up the blud-clat pussy-hole real good when we catch him. Me nah like that type of shit starr." Mugsy said. Sounding like Ox from the movie Belly 1.

Over the next couple of days me and Mugsy kept watch on Sayeed's house early in the mornings. So we could observe his movements when he came out of his house, and to also get a feel for his neighborhood in the early hours.

We needed to know what the foot traffic was like early in the mornings. We needed to know about these type of things before we made our move on him. A smart robber always did their scouting report to avoid surprises mid-robbery

Early in the morning about 4AM on December 30th, I got the call from Mugs.

"What's up rude boy, you ready to roll?" He asked, with out any preamble.

"Nah man today is Brittney's birthday, and I plan on staying on bed with her this morning and making love to my wifey then spending the day with her."

"Starr, I'm already outside your crib and I need to make some loot. Tell you what, lets switch cars since it's your girls birthday, you can chill with her in my Benz, while I use your van to check some shit out."

"Alright, we can do that, just give me a couple minutes to put some clothes on and I'll be outside." I said, ending the call.

After Mugsy had been gone with my van for about two hours, he calls me again "Rude boy I'm outside your crib, and I need to talk to you it's important." He said, concern evident in his voice.

When I go outside I find him sitting in my van looking a little shaken up and I ask "What's wrong with you my youth?"

"Starr, shit is all fucked up. I went by that Arab dude's crib and when I saw him coming outside I backed him down in front of his building. When I tried to take him back inside he started struggling and screaming. I ended up knocking his ass out cold so he would shut the fuck up and not wake up the whole neighborhood. I fucked him up real good before I left. He didn't have any money on him, all he had was this leather bag with papers in it. I took his house keys and I'm going to go back there to find the money when things cool down. You coming with me?"

"Nah that's a rap. I ain't going back over there."

I could not say I was surprised that Mugs had went to do my robbery without me. Brooklyn was full of cut-throat dudes. Friends were always double crossing each other, and I had did the same thing to him with the robbery in Connecticut, so I couldn't even get mad.

Enemies Amongst Us   D. Isaac

"Yo, you kicked his as real good?" I asked, trying to find the silver lining.

"Yeah, I pistol whipped his ass and left him out cold on the sidewalk."

"Did anyone see you?"

"Nah, ain't nobody seen me."

"Alright rude boy, good looking out for the ass whooping you gave him. I know Marilyn will be happy to hear he got that. It's to bad we didn't get his bread to though."

"Yo Dex, I'ma need my car back. I'm gonna go chill with my wife also, and you can give Black his gun back, I don't need it anymore I bought this browning 9mm." He said handing me the .38 revolver

"Alright Mugs, I'll get with you tomorrow." I told him, as we swapped car keys again.

After Mugsy had left I called Marilyn, "Bonjour, Cherrie." I started the conversation when she answered.

"Good morning" She replied sleepily then added "Why are you waking me up this early in the morning Dee?"

"I'm just calling to start your day with some good news, that business with Sayeed had been taken care of."

"What happened Dee?" she asked, sounding completely awake now.

"I took care of it like I told you I would. He got his ass kicked real good."

"I hope your not playing with me Dee, do you have any proof you robbed him?"

"Yeah I got his leather bag with some papers in it.?"

"Bring it to my house I want to see it?"

"Alright, I'll be up there in couple of hours", i replied, ending the call.

After I got off the phone with Marilyn, I called Black, "what's up playboy? I got your burner back and I want to return it to you this morning." I explained

"Did Mugsy kill anybody with it?" He asked understandably.

"Nah, he ain't kill nobody."

"Did ya'll handle that business for Marilyn?"

"Yeah, he got fucked up and robbed this morning. Yo, what time you want me to bring this thing back?"

"I don't want it back. Mugs probably put a body on that shit, so you can keep it or get rid of it."

"Alright then, I'ma get rid of it. I'll holla at you later." I told him and hung up.

Enemies Amongst Us   D. Isaac

Chapter 34

    Brittney could not get the day off from work ,so we had to change our plans of spending her birthday together. While watching her get ready for work, I got turned on just by looking as she lotioned her body and stood in our bedroom wearing her matching Victoria's Secrets bra and panty set.

    I got up out of bed, slid behind her, pulled her panties to the side and slid up in her. Giving her some early morning birthday sex before she went to work. There was nothing sexier than watching a woman get dressed first thing in the morning, especially knowing she was going out there to make money and bring it back to the family.

    After out morning quickie, she left to drop off the baby with the sitter on her way to work. Since I did not have anything to do until later on I decided to head up to Long Island to give Marilyn Sayeed's bag.

    As soon as I left my house, I hadn't drive a couple of blocks before I realized I was being trailed. I had a sixth sense for this type of shit. I'd spotted the mini van parked on the corner as I left my house, and I knew it didn't belong in my neighborhood as I'd never seen it parked there before.

    When your in the game, a street savvy hustler pays close attention to his surroundings at all times, especially to the surroundings he resides in.

    When I looked in my rear view mirror, I spotted two white men inside of the van and automatically knew right away they were the

Enemies Amongst Us   D. Isaac

police and they were after me.

I just kept on driving normally and heading for the Belt Parkway Highway. just before you get to the highway, there was a diner on Rockaway Ave. that had a drive around parking lot in it, I drove right into the parking lot of the diner and drove out the other side and headed on to the Belt as the light changed. Leaving the cops that were chasing me stuck and waiting for it to turn green again.

Once I got on the Parkway, I noticed a second vehicle following me, a tan Acura Legend, driven by a middle aged blonde white lady. She made the mistake of speaking on her walkie talkie while I was watching her in my mirror.

When I got to Queens I decided to run a test to see if I was not just being paranoid, I exited at the J.F.K. Airport exit, and sure enough I saw the Acura exit also, followed closely by the mini-van that had caught up. I followed the service lane known as the Conduit for the Belt, and jumped right back on the highway the first chance I got.

All typed of thoughts were going through my head as I was being followed by all kinds of cops. I was doing so much crime I didn't know which one they were after me for. All I knew was that I did not want to go to jail and I had to loose them quickly.

I called Mugsy, "Yo starr, some beast are following me on the highway. I"m going to shake them in you neighborhood. I need you to open up your garage and when I drive in close the door back down real quick."

"Alright rude boy, I got you, just make sure you shake them before you get to my crib." He said, ending the call.

Enemies Amongst Us   D. Isaac

When I pulled up to Mugsy's house the garage door was still closed, so I drove around the corner from his house, parked my van, and walked around the corner towards his house.

As I was walking Mugsy drove up in his Benz, I jumped in the back seat and laid down, and he drove off.

When I peeped up over the car seat and looked out the window, I see the blond hair woman in the Acura parking he car on the corner, as she looked around talking into a walkie talkie.

"Yo, just keep on driving." I told Mugs. He had seen the lady also and didn't need any more encouragement to get the hell out of there.

"Where you want to go?"

"Jump on the Southern State Parkway and head up to Long Island, I got to go see Marilyn."

Marilyn lived in a white, three level, split house, in the village of Hempstead.

The first thing out of Mugsy's mouth when we pulled up to her crib was, "Yo, this is the house she is going to sell you? You are a lucky mutha fucka Dex."

I was so busy admiring the house, I didn't pay attention to the jealousy that was radiating off of him.

Once inside the house I could see that Marilyn was about finished packing her stuff and ready to move out.

"Damn baby girl you ain't playing about getting out of here I see." I said, as we walked in.

"Yeah Dee, I'm out of here next week, and you can move in anytime after I leave."

"Oh yeah?"

"Yeah, once we get all the papers signed you and your family can move in."

"Alright ma, here is the bag I told you about." I said, handing her Sayeed's bag.

"I already saw it in your hand when you came through the door Dee. Just take it somewhere and burn it, make sure you get rid of it. I don't want it, I just wanted proof that you fucked him up."

"It's taken care of Cherri, he ain't going to be bothering you anytime soon."

****

After we left Marilyn's house I had Mugsy drive me by my apartment in Brooklyn. I wanted to see if the cops were watching my house. When we didn't see any around, I went inside to grab some money and Black's gun. Then I gave the gun to Mugsy and told him to drop me off at the Atlantic City Bus stop by the Kings Plaza Mall.

I needed to get out of the city to clear my head and figure this shit out. Once on the bus, I called Brittney at work and explained that I was going down to Atlantic City and for her to come down after she got off work. I told her how the cops had followed me when I left the house and that I thought it was a good idea to get out of the city and think for awhile. I even added that when she got down we'd celebrate her birthday.

Enemies Amongst Us					D. Isaac

My next call was to Pierre so he could reserve me a room at Bally's "What's up Dex, what's going on with you?" He asked, once I'd been patched through to his private line.

"I'm on my way down there my man, and I need a room."

"Dee it's New Years weekend and we're booked to capacity. Fuck there isn't a single room available in the whole city right now. I can put you on stand by in case somebody cancels, or the next time a room comes available. In the mean time you can stay at my apartment.

"Pierre I'm going to need a room because Brittney is coming down here to meet me. It's her birthday and I have to celebrate it with her."

"Alright let me see what I can do. Hopefully by the time she gets here a room will become available."

"Okay playboy, work your magic and I'ma see you when I get down there." I told him, ending our call.

I had forgot to grab another coat when I went back to my house, and had left the one I was wearing in my van when I jumped out in Queens to elude the cops.

By the time I got to Pierre's house in Atlantic City, I was coming down with a cold. I didn't have a single change of clothes with me and I was starting to feel miserable. My whole day had been fucked up from the time my phone woke me up at 4:30 AM.

Despite his best efforts Pierre couldn't get me a room that night and I had to stay at his crib. Brittney was not going to drive down because she couldn't find a sitter, and Pierre had a New Years Eve

Enemies Amongst Us   D. Isaac

party to go to, so I just laid on his bed and went to sleep praying things would be better when I woke up in the morning.

****

The following morning Pierre hit me about a room. He had conned one of his co-workers into giving me a nice suite and I was checked and settled in by 2 PM.

Still uneasy about the day before I decided to call my parole officer, to feel him out, and possibly see if this heat was coming from his office.

"Good morning Sir." I said politely after being transferred back to his office.

"Big man" He replied, like he was my homie or old friend.

"Yeah it's me." I replied, curious why he wouldn't use my real name.

"I need to see you." He started, sighed then continued, " I hear you've been running with a bad crowd."

"Does that have anything to do with why I spotted someone following me yesterday ?" I asked him, trying to get a handle on the severity of my situation.

"I have nothing to do with that Task Force." He replied, revealing the first , and only piece of information I needed to hear.

"Thanks Sir and enjoy the rest of your day, I will be in Wednesday to see you." I told him, ending the call.

After speaking with my Parole Officer, I knew my status had

Enemies Amongst Us   D. Isaac

nothing to do with the parole department, but rather a task force that was on to me. I quickly reasoned, that I was being surveyed because of the Africans I must of been seen associating with. The Nigerians in New York was doing so much fraud, the cops had put together a task force to take them down, and through my association with some of them, I had come under the radar of the task force, and now they was on to me.

What my parole officer did not tell me was, my so called friend Black had gotten busted buying stolen credit cards and had made a deal to cooperate with the Postal Police who was part of the task force, and had given me up to them. Nor did he tell me that my van was seen leaving the seen of a homicide the morning before.

Chapter 35

Knowing the cops were watching my every move had me spooked. Being on parole they knew where I lived, and I felt the need to shake Brooklyn A.S.A.P. Long Island was on the table I just had to wrap up that deal with Brittney and Marilyn.

About a week after my return from Atlantic City and getting a full understanding of what was going on Brittney and I took our son and moved from Brooklyn to the three bedroom Long Island home we'd bought form Marilyn.

Brittney and I had our new spot quickly laid out with new furniture and all the latest appliances. Everything was Gucci between us. Some mornings she would drop our baby off at the sitter before heading to work, or if she was running late I would do it before taking of on the hustle.

I told our neighbors I was in the music business so where they saw me dressed in casual clothing and carrying my briefcase they thought I was going to work in the office and thought nothing of it.

As time went by and I had not seen any police cars tailing me or anymore calls from the secret service, I once again let my guard down and went about business with no worries.

Little did I know I was sadly mistaken. Un-beknownst to me the Secret Service, NYPD, and the postal police, were now secretly investigating me, and they'd enlisted the help of Black and Michael Orasco.

It'd been months since the attempted Sayeed robbery, and I still

Enemies Amongst Us					D. Isaac

didn't know the true story. Turns out when I had called Black to return the burner he'd lend to Mugs, he called his handler from the postal police the second we had gotten off the phone. He told them Mugsy and I had committed the robbery and gave them Sayeed's name and address. The postal Police called the local police in Sayeed's district and told them about the possible robbery, also who did it.

That's when they replied that it was no longer a robbery investigation but rather a homicide. That was the point that all hell broke loose. Black's status as C.I. went up, and I was now under investigation for murder and I didn't even know it.

****

On May 20th of 1998 Marilyn returned from Paris after speaking to, and being tricked by NYPD homicide investigators. Upon her arrival at Kennedy International, she was arrested by the NYPD, and the Secret Service. She was later turned over to the custody of the US Marshalls Services and placed in the Metropolitan Detention Center on 29th St. in Brooklyn.

That was the same day I had taken Brittney to Radio City Music Hall to see Erykah Badu and Chico Debarge in concert. She had begged me all week to cancel my plans of going out of town to go to this concert with her. She had purchased the tickets months in advance and didn't want to go by herself. So like a model hubby, I canceled my trip and stayed in the city ,taking her to the show. Little did I know it would be the last concert I saw as a free man.

The night of the concert I left my truck in a 24 hours garage in Brooklyn, the one located on Atlantic and Grand Ave. I had rolled with Brittney in her Mercedes C280, so the next morning I'd have to get up early to catch a ride with her on her way to work.

As I was getting dressed that morning I got a call from Mugs "Yo Dex, the beast kicked in my door last night, but I wasn't there." He blurted, soon as I'd answered.

"What?" I said, not wanting to believe what he was telling me.

"Sheryl called me and told me the Feds kicked down our door at about 4 o'clock this morning looking for me, but I wasn't there." He repeated.

"Did they tell her why they were looking for you?" I asked, trying to gather any info and put the pieces together.

"Nah Starr, they didn't tell her anything, but they sure as shit scared the shit out of her and my kids, busting into my home so early in the morning."

"Damn Mugs, that's fucked up. Why you think they're looking for you?"

"I don't know brethren. It could be immigration, or a bunch of other shit. I been into all kinds of shit since I got back into the country."

"Alright man, let me get off this phone so I can get out of this house, I'ma hit you back when I get down to Brooklyn, I said, disconnecting the call.

That call form Mugsy had me spooked all over again. I quickly got myself, and the baby ready while Brittney was getting ready for work.

I stashed my guns in the safe, and grabbed some pocket money. I

Enemies Amongst Us
D. Isaac

couldn't help but feel like the walls were closing in on me from all directions. I couldn't wait to get outside, so I could see what kind of heat was on me. I had promised myself that I would never let the police put me in another cage. Suddenly I felt the urge to get the hell out of dodge every instinct in my body screaming to hit the road and drive.

"Brittney let me get your keys I want to drive." I demanded.

"Sure baby grab them out of my bag." She yelled back from the bathroom.

I was so deep in thought that when I left my house, I didn't notice the white panel van pull in behind me. When I reached the intersection of the corner of my house there was 4 police vehicles with Feds and Nassau police positioned around them. They all had their guns drawn and pointed in the direction of me and my family.

When I looked in my rearview mirror, I realized they had me boxed in. I could not reverse, and if I tried to drive around the cars in front I would either end up in the ditch or getting myself and my family shot. My son must've sensed something was wrong cause all of a sudden he started screaming and crying at that exact moment. When I looked over at Brittney she looked pale like she had just seen a ghost as she tried to calm our son down, she yelled out, "Dexter what did you do ? why are the cops pointing their guns at us ?"

"I haven't done anything Baby." I told her, trying to figure a way out of this situation.

When I was in prison I used to hear guys talking about, how they would rather hold court in the streets than come back to prison. I

Enemies Amongst Us   D. Isaac

had promise myself that I would never again let them put me back behind bars. All that went out the window, when I was staring down the barrels of 20 plus guns all aimed at me, my woman and my 1 year old baby, by a bunch of white men with a determined look on their faces. What a "G" is supposed to do ?

As all of these thoughts where racing through my head, I noticed one of the Cops come from behind his car, keeping his gun pointed at me, as he approached my side of the vehicle.

This was my chance to run his ass over and try to make a run for it or surrender. Brittney must of been sensing what I was thinking, because she reached over and squeezed my hand and whispered, "Don't do it Dee."

I just put the car in park and turned off the engine and surrendered after she said that. I could not risk Brittney and my son's lives, and the more I thought about it, I couldn't think of what they could charge me with anyway. Credit card and check fraud ? White collar crime ? A year, maybe two at the most. Boy was I in for a rude awakening.

I was taken to a building across the street from the World Trade Center in lower Manhattan. This was the New York City field office for the Secret Service, and I kept thinking to myself if Sayeed and his boys had succeeded in blowing up the Trade center, it would've fell on this building and probably killed some of these agents and possibly making my arrest impossible.

"Hello Dexter, my name is Special Agent Jack Bower and this is Detective Smith of the NYPD Homicide Division." This was the agent who had called me on my cell phone a while back, he said introducing himself and the other officer that was with him. " I

Enemies Amongst Us
D. Isaac

have been waiting a long time to talk to you."

"Oh yeah? I remember you telling me on the phone you wasn't going to arrest me." I said to him, feeling them out.

"Dexter, a lot have changed since then. You should of came and talked to me when I first called you, instead of getting that fancy Jewish shyster lawyer to call me." He said, with a smirk on his face.

"Okay, so tell me what have changed Mr. Secret Service agent man." I said, messing with him.

"Well for one, we are charging you with Murder now and credit card fraud, you should of came and talk to me before you stepped into the big leagues."

I sat there speechless after he said that. I kept thinking to myself these cops must of been crazy or they playing games, trying to scare me into working with them to take down the Nigerians. I know I didn't kill anybody, that was never my thing. I had robbed a lot of people, who were also criminals and in the game, but I didn't think any of them would incriminate themselves to tell on me.

I had even roughed up a few people in the process, but I had never killed anyone.

So I knew these cops must of been mistaken or tripping on something. I felt like I had nothing to worry about. So when they asked, Dexter are you ready to talk to us now ?"

I just looked at them and simply said, "I reserved the right to remain silent so nothing I say can't be used against me in a court of law, and I need to call my lawyer now please." Any smart street

Enemies Amongst Us   D. Isaac

soldier knows that will put an end to any interrogation they intend on starting.

After that they processed me and turned me over to the US Marshal Service at the Brooklyn Federal Courthouse. This is when it sunk in, and I knew shit was getting real. I found out I was officially getting indicted for Murder for hire, Robbery and credit card fraud.

After that, they read me my charges and rights again. I received a copy of my indictment and they escorted me to the Metropolitan Detention Center in Brooklyn, on 29th in Park Slope, where marilyn was already residing.

After I was proccess downstairs at MDC, they took me upstairs to a dormitory holding about 100 inmates. I started calling Brittney's phone to check up on her and our son, but she didn't answer. So I made the next call to my mother, and she informed me that they had arrested Brittney also. and they had brought the baby to her house.

The Cops were playing dirty because they knew Brittney had never committed a single crime in her life. She had nothing to do with my criminal lifestyle. She worked in a real-estate law firm from 9-5, went to school from 6-8 and was an active member in the Army Reserves, spending the first weekend of each month serving her country.

After they had drove off with me, the remaining cops had confiscated her car, then when she went back to the house to call a cab, more officers approached her requesting permission to search the house, even without a warrant.

Enemies Amongst Us   D. Isaac

Brittney was not a criminal and didn't have anything to hide, so she let them in after they threatened to stay put until the warrant arrived.

Upon searching the house the officers found numerous credit cards, fake ID's and counterfiet money. Also what appeared to be about 10 kilo's of crack cocaine. What they didn't know, was they'd actually found 10 kilo's of melted wax candles mixed with wheat flour to look like crack cocaine. They'd found my dummy batch that I used to rob suckers from out of town with.

After field testing it inside of the house a few times and it kept coming back negative for cocaine, confusing and frustrating the cops even more. Two of the offices decides to take some of it outside to test it in their vehicle, before coming back inside and claiming it popped positive all of a sudden.

They now had what they needed to charge Brittney with possesion of cocaine and they arrested her and put her in the hole(SHU) at the same detention center me and Marilyn were already at.

When I heard that they had arrested Brittney, I did what any real stand up "G" would do, I called my attorney and told him that everything in the house was mines, and Brittney had no knowledge of it.

I also mentioned that the drugs they found wasn't actually cocaine at all, but candle wax and flour, a fake. I took complete resposibilty for all of the contraband that was found in the house, again saying Brittney was clueless.

After my confession to my lawyer, he contacted brittney's lawyer

Enemies Amongst Us   D. Isaac

and told him that I was taking the rap. When she went to court the following week, she was released on $500,000 bail.

   At MDC Brooklyn, I met up with numerous homeboys that I had not seen in a while. I even met some new friends there as well. One day in the law Library, I ran into an old childhood friend Mad Max, Jimmy Henchman's right had man, that I grew up with,from back in the days when I lived in the Vanderveer Housing Projects in Flatbush.

"What's up Max ? What da hell you doing in here ?" I asked, surprised to see him in jail.

"Man you won't believe it Dex, if I told you ?" He said.

" Man, I taught you was down in Panama, chilling and shit."

" I was, until your man send the Feds down there to come get my ass."

"What da fuck you talking bout Max ?" I asked him, completely confused about who he was talking about.

" Dex, Jimmy called me on my cell phone down there with the Feds and they triangulated my phone and came and extradited me back up here man." He said, looking sad and stressed out.

"Yo Max, why would Jimmy do that to you ?" I asked, still not believing what he was saying to me.

"Dex man, one day we was down in Miami to buy some work, (Drugs) and Jimmy sent me to his hotel room to pick up $150,000 he had there, and when I went to get to get the money, I saw the Feds watching the hotel and I left. Some how the money came up

Enemies Amongst Us					D. Isaac

missing and he blamed me for taking it.

I couldn't believe my ears. Jimmy was suppose to be a stand up guy. Our childhood friend, he would never do something like that. I kept saying to myself. Naive to how shit went down in the Feds.

"Yo Max, what floor your on ? I asked, him changing the subject.

"Man I'm on the 4th floor with Pistol Pete and Mac 11, from the Sex Money Murder gang in the Bronx. I got Scooter from the 90's there with me as well and that Nigga King Tut from East New York. They got Jamaican Randy and Copper from Rutland Rd, on the 6th floor also. They got a bunch of niggas up in this bitch Dex."

Man it looked like they had a lot of the hustlers from all over the city up in this building." Yo Max from now on we is going to meet up here in the library every Wednesday so we can kick it. I'm on the 3rd floor underneath you." I told him, and went back down to my unit. I would go on to Meet Pistol Pete, Blue from Harlem, and a quit a few of the major players from the city up in the Library. I would become friends with Little Nicky a captian in the Gambino family, and Johnny Papa a young Italian Hitman from Brooklyn

It was about a year later when Marilyn and I went to trial at the Federal Court House in the Eastern District of New York in Brooklyn. It was during this trial that, I would learn the hard way, the sad truth that there was no more honor amongst thieves, or home boys keeping it real anymore. Those days were long gone. That breed extinct.

Five of my so called friends came to court during the course of my trial, all had cut deals to avoid prosecution. All took the stand and eventually lied about what we were doing together, thus

Enemies Amongst Us   D. Isaac

earning their freedom.

Mike the guy Carlos had talked me into letting stay at my stash house, when he was homeless went first. He was a paid government informant the whole time, going from state to state befriending hustlers and drug dealers and turning them over to the DEA and FDI for money to support his crack habit, he did such a stellar job they eventually provided him with a clothing store in the garment district of NYC. Talk about a misuse of tax payers funds.

Pierre had also gotten himself busted trying to do a cash advance with a stolen credit card he had begged me to give him, so he could get the rims for his car. he was facing a max of a 1 year sentence and he didn't even want to do one day in jail, so he decided to flip on me to avoid doing his time like a man.

Carlos had gotten himself busted on the the highway transporting drugs and testified against me to save himself also. his testimony hurt me the most, mainly because he was like a brother to me. When he pointed out my mother in the courtroom and admitted he calls her Ma, I felt like he pushed a dagger straight through my chest. My lawyer could feel the tension radiating off, of me so he grabbed my arm and whispered in my ear that I need to sit there and take it.

Mugsy dumb ass had got caught up after being on the run for a year just before my trial started. He got caught smoking weed in his car as he ran a red light in Florida.

At first he denied not knowing me or committing any crimes with me. But as soon as the Feds told him he would get immunity for all of the crimes he had committed in the United States and not get deported back to Jamaica if he were to help them and testify on me.

he flipped, and couldn't tell them enough. Mugsy told them about unsolved murders that they knew nothing about, and how he was shipping drugs from Jamaica to the US and then sending the money back to Jamaica, he even lied and told them it was me who killed Sayeed. Knowing damn well I was at home with Brittney and my son.

Just before my trial began, I heard about an eye witness to Sayeed's murder. A man named Jose Morales happened to be looking out of his window at about 5AM that fateful morning.

He had called 911, and when the police arrived he told them he had seen a 5'5", 150 pounds, black man with a short afro, dark complexion emerge from a van, and confront Sayeed before shooting him. Then getting back in the van and speeding away by himself.

The US Attorney, Agent Jack Bower, Detective Smith and my crooked Legal Aid lawyer, did everything they could to keep Mr. Morales from taking the stand in my defense.

I was convicted of Murder For Hire, Hobbs act Robbery, and possesion of a firearm, even though I was never caught with a gun. The final sentence was life plus 5 years. Marilyn was also convicted of Murder For Hire and Hobbs act robbery. She was sentenced to life in prison.

In April of 2000 after sentencing, I was flown up to the United States Penitentiary Leavenworth in the state of Kansas, and this is where my new life began as a federal prisoner.

At USP Leavenworth, I ran into a whole bunch of homies that I hadn't seen in a long time that was missing from New York. At

USP Leavenworth, I would also meet a lot of Gangsters and gang members from all over the country and from around the world. The place was like a big melting pot full of thugs. At USP Leavenworth is where "From Friends To Enemies and Enemies Amongst US " ends, and "When Enemies Becomes Friends " starts. Because I would learn that there is strength in numbers in prison. Stay tuned. The Saga continues. (:>)

The End.

Acknowledgements

 First and foremost I would like to give Praise to the King of Kings, Lord of Lords, The Conquering Lion of the Tribe of Juda Jah Rastafari, for keeping me sane and safe for the past 20 years, while I have been residing in the belly of the beast. I would also like to give thanks to my Lord and Savior Jesus Christ for teaching me all things is possible through him.

 I would like to thank my mother and best friend for loving me unconditionally and holding me down like a true Queen. I love you with all my heart Old Girl.(:>) I would like to thank the mother of my child, Michelle aka Queen Fatima aka my Eskimo Bunny (:>)for holding me down over these past 20 years. You had to be a father and mother to our son, and raise him by yourself. Thank you Babe for putting up with all of my madness, and never abandoning me when the going got ruff. You are my "Ride and Live" chick forever. They don't make them like you anymore Baby Girl. I will always love you for eternity and unconditionally with all of my heart.

 I would like to thank my brothers from another mother, Wayne Cham, it's always a pleasure to hear from you my dude. Big shout outs to Junior Cham for all the editing, formatting and book uploading y'all always put a smile on my face whenever I'm stressed da fuck out up in this bitch. I love you fellas. Y'all are the true definition of real friends. Shout out to the entire Champagnie family. Y'all been riding with me from day one. Shout out to Darrell Wilds aka Ice for always coming through for me when I need a few dollars. Love you cuz. What's up Bucky? We did it again Sis. I love you Baby Girl. Thanks for always having my back and coming through for me when I need you. The love is real.

Enemies Amongst Us					D. Isaac

I would like to thank my man Asher Underwood aka the Albino Gorilla and his beautiful wife Melissa for building me a fabulous website and always coming through for me when I need a book cover.. Man congrats on baby Kaya and know that I got mad love for you dude. I would also like to thank my main man, Pastor Lane Lewis and his wife Lady Allison, for riding with me from day one, and holding me down and sending me them daily words to give me inspiration on my cloudy days. Man you showed me GOD is Good.

Shout out to my cellie from the ATL zone 3 4 season, Hussain for keeping me feeling young and putting me up on that YFN Lucci, that 21 Savage and all that dirty south swag.

Shout out to Kory A. Hall for snapping me out of my writers block, and helping me finish this book. Watch out for his books coming soon people. Da boy got some heat coming, and you better believe it.

Shout out to all of the NYC Jack boys, and all of the Jack boys from all over the county and around the world. This one is for you. Haitian Jack, Rooster, Ricky Lee, Joker, Randy and Copper. Pistol Pete and Mac 11, Shoeshine, Rat, Peter Brown, Patrick and Erick Folks, the entire Folks Family, Kadien. Keep ya ski masks on and your guns loaded Rude Boys, and take that money from them suckas.(:>) Blaka blaka blaka, you know how we do.

Shout out to my man Kida from Fresno. For proof reading my book and always lending me an ear when I needed it. You are a real dude my bro. Shout out to my young partna Pree from Frisco for keeping me lit and giving me game on that IG stuff.

I would also like to give a shout out to some of the fellas I have been doing time with over the years. My DC partna Kevin Gray aka KG, Nehemiah aka Hampton El, Michael Davis aka 88, Wendell Smith aka Big Dog. My B-More partnas Mookie, Keyon, Tiger, Tony Bey, and Big Harry. My NYC Mob partna Johnny Papa, Chucky Russo, Anthony Senter, Tommy karate, Little Nicky and Big Nick. To my man Pimp from upstate hanging out with my over here at FCI Mendota. To my Northern Family partna Choppa and my Fresno Bulldogg partna Big Noey and Gangster. To my man Dre for helping me fight my case and all of the typing and time in that law library. I can't thank you enough man.

Last but not least, if you did not see your name in these acknowledgements it's not that I forgot about you, it's just that you forgot about me. Just know that I love you all the same.

Made in the USA
Columbia, SC
04 January 2020